The Bible,
the Bomb,
the Burden

A faith-based look at the full truth
of God and how modern science came to
overshadow the church; a suggested way
to approach widening generation gaps

John E. Eash

ISBN 978-1-0980-9790-5 (paperback)
ISBN 978-1-0980-9791-2 (digital)

Christian Faith Publishing, Inc.
832 Park Avenue
Meadville, PA 16335
www.christianfaithpublishing.com

Printed in the United States of America

Contents

Important: Please Read

This book is about the creative presence of Jesus Christ in our universe in a way the church and most theology do not address. I propose the words "perfect truth" to define this concept and to lift up areas where I believe we need to pursue it further. Although it is humanly impossible to fully grasp what all that completely means, the fulness of the Trinity provides the assurance of his omnipresence, omniscience, and omnipotence. Because the scope of the words "perfect truth" is so far-reaching, there is further definition and some examples in the text. The word *perfect* is intended in the way it involves God's eternal purposes and the references to perfection and completion in the New Testament. Jesus confirms a complete gospel at Calvary in his last words, "It is finished" (John 19:30). Paul confirms it in what is called the love chapter. He admits there are gaps in our knowledge now and some things we can't explain. But the day is coming when it will be clear as crystal (1 Cor. 13:9–10). In the meantime, this "perfect truth" sustains our universe.

"Thanks be to God for his unspeakable [indescribable] gift" (2 Cor. 9:15).

Preface

One thing seems to be true; there is not now—and never has been—a consensus on how to judge perfect truth. This book offers another approach.

This book is written as a faith-based effort to help the church of Jesus Christ examine fresh ways to bring the gospel to a rapidly changing world. It stems from my own trust in Jesus Christ and what he has done for me and doubtless gives many clues about my own beliefs. It is not to compare or comment on other beliefs; there is only one gospel (Gal. 1:6–9). You will see that my thesis actually encourages all of us to seek more ideas on how to apply the Bible to present-day society in every culture. On one hand, we live in the same flesh-and-blood world as all the people who were on earth when the Bible was being recorded, which we all can understand. On the other hand, if Moses, Abraham, Isaiah, Peter, or Paul stepped out of a time capsule into a modern city, they would think they discovered another planet. If Miriam, Sarah, Mary, Lydia, or Martha could step into a modern kitchen, they would think they were having hallucinations.

Over twenty centuries ago, a Greek mathematician named Archimedes said, "Give me a lever long enough and a fulcrum on which to place it, and I shall move the world." Two hundred years later, God made it possible, and ever since then, the church has had that power: standing on Christ the solid rock, the Bible our lever, and the fulcrum a hill called Calvary.

Humanity has been lost ever since Adam and Eve were evicted from the Garden of Eden. Since then, our only salvation is eternal life as it is proclaimed in the New Testament. What looms large over every page of this book, though, is the shadow of this world's god. He is relentless and fearless as he convinces millions that they can find all the blessings they need without the church. I personally don't believe that many of them are aware they are headed away from God. I have never heard anyone say, "I don't want to go to heaven." They just don't know. They are sheep without a shepherd, and a wolf hides in plain sight pretending that all the blessings we enjoy are gifts from his world. They don't know that Jesus called his bluff when he kept faith during the temptation: "Man does not live by bread alone," "Thou shalt not tempt the Lord thy God," "Thou shalt worship the Lord thy God, and him only shalt thou serve" (Matt. 4:4, 7, 10).

Teaching and Learning Pattern Changes

Things this book does not do: It does not mean to comment on your personal faith—to do so would seriously interfere with its real intent. Neither does it suggest a unity of doctrines, interpretations, or practices among believers. Another thing it does not mean to imply is that the theme of "balance" has anything to do with weighing or judging sins. "For by grace are ye saved through faith" (Eph. 2:8). It does offer you a plain invitation to read the Bible through the eyes of your own faith while considering all the knowledge available in this century. You will see, as you read, that there are two connected themes: First, that no matter what we believe or think about anything that exists, the whole truth is always found in the acting presence of Jesus. Second, that seventy-five years ago, traditional beliefs began to hold us back from understanding the world in an Atomic Age. Our various theologies, that is, the way we interpret God's Word and shape doctrines and faith statements, had been tested and tried over many generations. This means you and I are the beneficiaries of faith that has held firm for centuries. The results of our firmness, though, have been contributing to our widening generation gaps as new discoveries add new spiritual problems. If you are led to agree with any of the truths offered in this book, I hope they will help you seek ways to look for fresh connections. The generations need bridges now. If nothing else, I encourage discussion and sharing ideas within your own circle.

We need to look deeper into the Word of God than we have historically, at least as far as I understand it. Modern technology has progressed beyond some of our traditional areas of thought. The thoughts are fine in themselves, but science has taken us beyond time-honored thought patterns. Connecting with the learning patterns of today's generation might be easier if we can adapt to Jesus's style. Traditional Western education has relied on taking the time to reason things out, look at all factors involved, see how they fit together, observe cause and effect, and draw conclusions. Jesus taught according to the custom of his day—show-and-tell style. Look at the different sides of a subject, turn it this way and that, and see how it looks from different angles. They couldn't take notes. Jesus gave picture-thoughts they could retain. The kingdom is like a treasure in a field. It is like a pearl of great price. It is like a net. It is like a pan of dough. It is within you. You enter into it. It is at hand. How can

I describe these people? They are like children complaining that they aren't getting their way. They have hard hearts and blocked ears and blind eyes (Luke 13:19–21; Matt. 13:15, 44–47). As time passed, the New Testament was added to the Old Testament. Then the church learned how to translate everything into modern written language that most could understand. Today though, the written language is going through another transformation and is taking the younger generations with it. Our ancient Bible truths need to be brought back to life again for people whose learning patterns have changed.

I expect that you, the reader, may have questions or wonder about certain conclusions that I have made. That is one reason for this entire effort. In any moment of time, there are questions no one can answer, and differences that cannot be humanly resolved. But if you and I together can agree to love each other, persuade others, and confess that sometimes only God knows, then perhaps we will really see more glory of God's kingdom in our own day. We come together with our humanly understood "truths." We share them in the light of God's Word. Where there are areas or opinions that do not seem to agree, we confess that Jesus is the Way, the Truth, and the Life (John 14:6). We live out the gospel—with our personal faith statements—as the Holy Spirit leads.

"For we know in part, and we prophesy in part. But when that which is perfect is come, then that which is in part shall be done away" (1 Cor. 13:9–10).

1
Introduction

A biblical irony: One of the last questions ever directed to Jesus was by Pilate. Jesus said, "Everyone that is of the truth heareth my voice." Pilate replied, "What is truth?" and walked away (John 18:37–38). The poor fellow didn't recognize truth when it was staring him in the face through the person of Jesus Christ. You may have heard this truth stated before.

A current irony: After two thousand years of exhaustive study, Christians, as well as the Pilates of today, are still struggling with the same question: What is truth? Their struggling, rather than producing an answer, has produced numerous definitions. These definitions have produced countless divisions among people, and now there are whole populations arguing over this same old question, "What is truth?" My conclusion is that, if we accept that truth as truth is the literal presence of Jesus Christ (i.e., He is the Way, the Truth, and the Life), we will grasp the fact that words alone can never fully define truth. Truth is more than words can tell. As I explain my thesis, I will show how a scientific paradox illustrates the point.

This book is an effort to help the church of Jesus Christ examine fresh streams to bring living water to our rapidly changing, but still thirsty, world. Humanity has been lost, trying to find its own way, ever since Adam and Eve were evicted from the garden of Eden. As believers, we find that our way to salvation is through the finished work of Jesus Christ, who shed his blood at Calvary for the remissions of sins. Fueling the perpetual struggle between good and evil is Satan's ability to persuade humanity that it can regain Eden's blessings on its own. Now, the realities of computers' artificial intelligence, gene-splicing, and social media are raising old questions of morality in a modern setting. The Bible continues to offer our best guidance on how to relate God's truths to this conflicted society. "My help cometh from the Lord, which made heaven and earth" (Ps. 121:2). "For the weapons of our warfare are not carnal but mighty through God to the pulling down of strong holds" (2 Cor. 10:4). The Bible stands.

"One Lord, One Faith, One Baptism" (Eph. 4:5–6)

After two thousand years of effort, the church is failing to produce a unified witness to the Gospel. The gulf between conservative and liberal schools of thought prevents them from reaching out to each other despite sincere devotion to the same God and Christ, trusting to the guidance of the same Holy Spirit, and seeking truth in the same Holy Bible. Extreme differences of opinion have—at worst—resulted in shooting wars and inquisitions. Claiming to follow Jesus who is the Way, the Truth, and the Life has given permission to conduct physical violence against those who have a competing truth. In modern friendlier times, there are efforts by some groups to find grounds for cooperation on friendly terms, both in local community settings as well as at national levels. But even in many of these situations, there is a lack of fully trusting the conclusions of others. The deep-seated grip of long-held convictions brings up fears of relaxing one's hold on what is held to be a life-saving doctrine. Conflicted feelings are feared as a possible evidence of unfaith. Then there are other groups content to go their own way, following their individual theological perceptions of gospel, truth, and so on. By themselves within the church, we can see these differences of opinion as family squabbles. Some members of the family get along better than others. Some not at all. Some feel that others are not holding on to established family values. Some actively compete through sibling rivalries. Not only does this result in a loss of energy and material resources, it also produces a blunted witness of the good news and to the critical eye of the world around us. It gives them a blurry picture of a house divided against itself.

2
Truth

Definition: According to Colossians 1:15–20, Jesus is the truth who reconciles everything in God's creation to himself. In John 14:6, Jesus says, "I am the Way, the Truth, and the Life." The words *way, truth,* and *life* are often used in a general sense, sometimes interchangeably, when referring to this verse. As a phrase they stand out because they emphasize Jesus's mission, teaching, and example. They are valuable descriptions of who he is, but without some explanation, it is hard to draw a mental picture of their meaning. Jesus as the Truth is omnipotent, omniscient, and omnipresent—all-powerful, all-knowing, and everywhere present.

God has given us timeless all-encompassing truth in Jesus, who truly is the Way, the Truth, and the Life. Most believers concur with that statement in a general sense. My belief is that scientific breakthroughs in the last century have opened a brand-new dimension to that belief. As total sum and substance of all truths, Jesus literally represents perfect truth. In the person of omnipresent God, he is the constructive presence in the entire universe in a way the church and theology overlook. We have always had descriptions of perceived truth, ancient truth, moral truth, truth observed with the five senses, all defined by our human knowledge, experience, and understanding. But no matter how much we try to explain it, the meaning and value of

100 percent pure "truth" in any statement, proposition, opinion, or doctrine depends on how closely they measure up to the perfect truth of Jesus Christ.

Applications of perfect truth, as our main topic, will be to our whole known universe plus infinity. Moreover, since nothing exists free from the influence of perfect truth, the use of the term in these pages is merely one example. Various subjects are connected with natural laws of our physical world, including the dimension of time plus our invisible "nonmaterial" world, relating all of it to truth and basing it on faith. Since we are all different, you and I perceive the truths of faith through our private individual senses. Human minds and reasoning can never fully surround or contain all truth on this side of eternity. This book will consider how perfect truth is over, under, around, and through everything.

Definitions of Truth

Everybody has a knowledge of truth in one way or another. Some we acquire on our own, and some we learn as others teach us. We don't know what we don't know. Research and development have become a huge part of science and industry because there is so much more to learn, and they keep coming up with new ideas. Also, perceptions of truth will vary among different cultures from one part of the world to another, as well as in the gaps between generations.

Essays, in recent years, describe how truth changes in the thinking of people over time. In reality, truth is basically only our perception of what the facts really are. Truth today depends upon "where you are coming from" and many other definitions. There no longer is a clear-cut meaning for the truth of any proposition today. As beauty is in the eye of the beholder, so truth is likewise defined by the senses and perceptions of the observer.

Since this is a theological discussion of all truths and not about language and grammar, I begin with several Bible texts as framework for the whole subject. There are other passages that could also serve. These are fairly familiar and usually accepted as important. So they are not exclusive, but every journey needs a stepping-off point. The reader may have selected others. All quotations are from the King James Version.

1. Jesus said, "I am the Way, the Truth, and the Life." This is the basic text for the thesis of this book. The Way and the Life are cradled in perfect truth. Therefore, if we follow in the Way, we will discover perfect truth which is and always will be Life. Jesus Christ is the same yesterday, today, and forever. (Heb. 13:8) We must come to him to find life. It is more than relying on printed words alone. "Search the scriptures; for in them ye think ye have eternal life: and they are they which testify of me. And ye will not come to me, that ye might have life" (John 5:39–40).

2. A mountain peak of John's Gospel speaks to our human predicament. God provides the only way of salvation as his love harmonizes our spiritual and material needs (John 3:16:).

3. The two greatest commandments, to love God and love your neighbor, although not mentioned often, are established as indispensable signposts along the Way and are fundamental.

4. The living and active double-edged sword—the Word of God—that divides even the soul and

spirit, joints, and marrow and judges the attitudes of the heart (Heb. 4:12).

The Main Statement

As mentioned in the introduction, my thesis on finding real truth is based on a well-known paradox. A paradox is a statement that may seem contradictory but may be true, or a statement that is self-contradictory and, therefore, false. The paradox is "What happens when an unstoppable force meets an immovable object?" The truth seems to be that there is no answer because it can never happen and can't be demonstrated. If the force stops, it is not unstoppable. If the object moves, it is not immovable. My conclusion is that the point where the two meet is pure truth and that science hasn't found it yet. It's a spiritual question. Perfect truth is where they meet in the middle and balances the back and forth reciprocating energy waves from within them. There has been some thought that this paradox can only happen if a deity is involved. To me, there is no "if." There is nothing now or that has ever been or ever will be anything where God is not involved.

Newton's third law: For every action, there is an equal and opposite reaction—a pair of forces acting on the interacting objects. The "pair of forces" is perfect truth working toward balance.

Truth is also found at the perfect center of a dilemma when you must choose between two alternatives. It may mean picking one of two favorites or could be choices that are unpleasant, sometimes called choosing the lesser of two evils. We say "stuck between a rock and a hard place," "it's do or die," "choosing a fork in the road," "you can't have your cake and eat it too."

"Choose you this day whom ye will serve" (Josh. 24:15).

Sometimes the truth is clouded from lack of knowledge or confusing signals.

While these definitions may seem wordy or repetitious, don't worry about memorizing them. This book has nothing to do with the worn-out debates over moral relativism. That is, moral standards of right and wrong depend upon what you feel they are. There are no moral truths. That position, of course, ignores the Bible. "When he, the Spirit of truth is come, he will guide you into all truth" (John 16:13).

This book claims the following: Every truth we can think of and the sum total of all truths comes from, and eternally exists in, the life and actions of Jesus Christ. *Perfect truth*, as his creative presence, takes part in every thought and action and is totally present within every living creature and all inanimate objects. As one with the omnipotent, omniscient, omnipresent God, he exists in every moment of time and measure of space carrying out God's will. It is to lift up perfect truth as the living interface between all truths, the reciprocating action between all opposing forces, and the perfect balancing point for every and all truths. Further, it is likely impossible for two individuals ever to completely see truths in the same way or to have identical faiths. Perfect truth is the meeting place between faith and doubt, the perfect solution for every controversy, and the answer to every riddle. God's plan seeks perfect balance in everything, from the rotation of the earth to the nerves and muscles in your body while you are trying to be comfortable as you are reading this book.

Examples of the reciprocating action of the power of perfect truth seeking perfect equilibrium between opposing forces:

➤ In the material world, we recognize this as energy and motion.
  • Irresistible force and an immovable object.
  • Swinging pendulum.
  • Teetering seesaw, riding a bike.
  • Water versus water wheel.
  • Hammer driving nail.
  • An object in motion tends to remain in motion. An object at rest tends to remain at rest.
  • Vibration in a hummingbird's wings.
  • Pistons in an engine.

➤ In the nonmaterial spiritual realm and relationships, we use other language for differing opinions, conflicted emotions.
  • Follow your head or your heart.
  • When does a holy concern become a worry?
  • Human-divine relationship
  • I'm firm in my convictions. You're stubborn.
  • Love-hate relationships—personality conflicts.
  • Where is the perfect center of their truths in a parent-child argument?
  • Balancing a budget, balancing one's time.
  • What is the ideal size for a congregation?
  • What color should we paint the fellowship hall?
  • Which job should I take?
  • Faith meets reason.
  • Predestination and self-will.
  • Judgment calls: at the county fair, which is the best jelly, canned vegetables, quilt, baked goods, animal, etc.?

- When is the cake baked to perfection?
- The reciprocal blessing in giving and receiving a gift.

Ad infinitum—perfect truth has been actively present since Genesis 1. (John 1:1–3)

One area discussed will deal with visible, solid facts, actions, and things we can test with our five senses. Other areas will consider invisible facts like thoughts, emotions, and other feelings with their spiritual effects.

3
God's Plan—Humanity's Fall

The Center of "SIN" Is "I"

Ever since the fall and expulsion from the garden of Eden, human beings have been trying desperately to regain their lost paradise. Born without the ability to live sin-free lives, we live in an imperfect world cursed by the sin we share. The whole Bible is a record of the kinds of things that have happened in the past and still do today simply because nothing has changed. We are born with the desire to have a meaningful life. We are all carrying a sign that says "I want to feel important." The first murder is a prime example of what can happen when this feeling gets out of hand: Cain killed Abel because HE wanted to be number 1 in God's eyes. As believers, we know that Jesus came into the world to offer us a way out of this doomsday scenario. Recognizing Jesus as perfect truth enables us to see around and through the liar and father of lies who speaks every language in the world.

The failure of human efforts to create a peaceful world free of hate, greed, and strife is because all such intentions—without God's help—simply combine our fatal flaws. This is why Paul warns us not to be misled by the doomed philosophies of this world. They cannot rise above the highest level of human reasoning (Col. 2:8). You can't serve up a good breakfast omelet with rotten eggs. The Bible shows us, in plain words, what goes wrong: Men try to get to heaven with their own schemes. (You may want to stop and read about the Tower of Babel now. It takes only a minute and a half [Gen. 11:1–9].) Apparently, they all understand the project. With no reference to God, "the children of men" planned to build a city with a watchtower reaching to heaven. Then, whenever they wanted to, they would be able to climb up to the top and be able to see the whole world. They would be really proud of themselves because they'd reached heaven on their own. Their human efforts would give them a name they never had before, and their spirit of unity and purpose would be preserved if all can stay within their own self-imposed limits. They were perverting the real reason why God showed them how to make bricks.

Because basic human nature has never changed, it is kind of curious that there seems to be a special status given to the tallest building in a city. From time to time, the news reports that a certain country has just completed the tallest building in the world. The item usually hints at an unspoken competition for the distinction. This can include adding the height of communication antennae on the roof depending on who is keeping score.

Human Schemes are Fruitless

Along with our inherited sinful nature, we are heirs of a creation that left to itself is headed for its eventual ruin. This is often said to follow the second law of thermodynamics, which deals with the subject of energy. One example of this theory is the subject of freezing and melting. Set an ice cube out at room temperature, and it will melt. You can sit there and wait forever, but it will never refreeze itself. Other examples patterned after this idea are that everything there is will wear out, spoil, get dirty, rust, fall apart, or break. If leftovers spoil, they will never unspoil. Rusty tools will never unrust. Dirty clothes don't wash themselves. A broken chair won't repair itself. Spilled jelly beans will not gather themselves together and spill back into the jar. Bear in mind that the law mentioned here has not actually been proven. It does apply as the principle in air-conditioning and refrigeration. This same principle applies to personal circumstances: Hunger can't feed itself, and thirst can't quench itself; they need ongoing nourishment. Friendships need to be maintained, or they tend to wither. Love needs to be expressed or renewed in one way or another, or it tends to fade. The other side of this coin never seems to change either. Rot, rust, filth, brokenness, hunger, confusion, hate, grudges, and other unsavory things never go away by themselves and tend to get worse. This negative unproductive state occurred long before there were theories, philosophies, or laws discovered by human beings. The world we have been born into was cursed by God.

The Bible tells us that after Adam and Eve spoiled their perfect world by disobedience, the Lord God said to Adam, "Cursed is the ground for thy sake; in sorrow shalt thou eat of it all the days of thy life...in the sweat of thy face shalt thou eat bread, till thou return unto the ground; for out of it wast thou taken: for dust thou art, and unto dust shalt thou return" (Gen. 3:17, 19). So he drove out the man and placed at the east of the garden of Eden cherubim and a flaming sword which turned every way to keep the way of the tree of life. (Gen. 2:17–19) To this day, the same tempter who got them thrown out, the god of this world, has been successfully convincing men, women, and youth that he has keys to help them get back in through another way.

Our Mission Sorely Needed

Our lost world's only "perpetual motion" since the fall in the garden of Eden is the battle between good and evil, life and death. Spiritual wickedness from hell and the rulers of darkness assumed their new jobs right out of the garden gate. Even now, they are at work dragging everything down with them. Scripture makes it plain: Our only hope is in Jesus Christ, the Way, the Truth, and the Life. In the fullness of time, God reset the button at Calvary. It's as though we are on a sinking ship, and he is the one who came from heaven to save us (John 3:13).

Even though I have only included sample references, the text for this project is the whole Bible, God's recorded Word. These scripture references are arbitrary choices. You, the reader, may prefer others. Using the whole Bible avoids taking certain scriptures out of context that can lead to misinterpretation. Think of the Bible as God's website with links to related pages. Some links are used more often than others. My choice for home page is John 3:16. If, as it's been said, the Bible is a word from eternity, then it is the best word capable of describing eternal truth. For this entire work, it's fair to say that any commentaries, axioms, derivatives, and conclusions that are not directly scripture quotes are like a treasurer's report: heard as given and filed, subject to audit.

It would seem that the Bible has become irrelevant as far as having any real influence in present-day society. Some believers regard this falling away over a period of time as positive because it confirms conditions of the end times. Others see it as negative because it means we are losing ground in our continuing struggle with evil. Either way, for the gospel's sake and its mission in the world, it's time for all the body of Christ to pull the same direction in proclaiming the gospel while we "work out our own salvation with fear and trembling" (Phil. 2:12). Regardless of how you may value the urgency of this project, I feel that God's perfect truth has been involved in the whole situation according to his perfect plan. The author takes the responsibility for errors, lack of clarity, and every idle word (Matt. 12:36).

4
Truth in Different Settings

Even if we were able to reach total agreement on the meaning of words and their usage, there is still the issue of what they mean in different situations. Truth, as our main topic, includes every meaning given in every dictionary in every language. Looking for the truth in a court of law is different from looking for truth in the way a caterpillar turns into a butterfly.

Here is one example of how truth is treated in a court of law: Justice is to be blind to distractions and intended to dispense fairness. The oath assumes you will tell the truth, the whole truth, and nothing but the truth. Actually, it all will be only perceived truth. One person sees it from this angle, another from that angle, and both of them are trying to be honest. Each juror and the judge hear it from "where they are sitting" (literally, as well as mentally and spiritually). Probably more than one has prayed for divine guidance in separating truth from falsehood. Then, when the case rests, a verdict is declared based on a refined mixture of combined truths, the truths as perceived by lawyers, witnesses, the judge, and twelve individual jurors. The verdict of composite truths that has been reached allows the accused to go free or be detained for sentencing. Perfect truth has been balancing and guiding toward an outcome in harmony with God's long-term plans for the world. Judge, jury, and accused may or may not agree that justice has been done. As believers in perfect truth, we allow room for the many new truths to which we are constantly exposed. They cannot be ignored. And since Jesus is the same yesterday, today, and forever, he is constantly involved with the timely appearance of these truths and all other conceivable definitions of perfect truth that may yet appear.

Truth Has Many Facets

There is differing truth in the meanings we give to some things. Just two examples are "the meaning of things lies not in the things themselves but in our attitude toward them" (Antoine de Saint-Exupéry) and "there are many truths of which the full meaning cannot be realized until personal experience has brought it home" (John Milton). There is truth in symbols (i.e., the pattern on a piece of material known as a flag). No definitions can be omitted if we really want to know the truth. Take into consideration that even though definitions of truth remain constant in print, the meanings of some words change over time. The meaning of a paragraph may change when read over a lapse of centuries. Even translating something into another current language has the same risk. The little Italian girl says, "I was taught that *burro* [butter] is something to spread on my bread. Now, here in Spanish class, they tell me it is something to ride." Translating Hebrew or Greek into German, Italian, Chinese, and African languages can never produce identical words and grammar. Even today's European languages make a distinction between male, female, and neuter nouns and pronouns. A major point of this book is that because beliefs and conscience are limited by individual lessons learned, life experience, and natural intelligence, understandings of perfect truth will always vary between individuals even when using identical words. Truth can have many definitions. For example, in this statement, "the sky is blue," the truth is obvious. Just look up. Or is it? What if it is a rainy day? What about a blind person, or a child who has not learned his/her colors yet? What if you understand there really is no "sky" and the "blue" is really an optical phenomenon that is merely described differently in these instances?

Jesus said, "I am the Way, the Truth, and the Life." We understand that in this three-fold description, Jesus gives us attributes of himself even though the three words are nouns. The words are often blended when using the verse as a sermon text or in Bible study. That is not a problem, though, since we take them to be qualities in his person. As a phrase, they stand out because they are the substance of Jesus's missions, teaching, and example. He does not say, "If you want to go to heaven, follow the GPS, obey the Ten Commandments, and be sure to recalculate when so instructed, and you should be all right." Instead, as the Way, he walks beside us and points out the signposts along the path. As perfect truth, he leads us in the narrow way that cuts through temptations of the world's evil, showing us the difference between truth and lies. As Life, he dwells within us, spiritually enabling us to live a holy, fulfilling life continuing into eternity. Therefore, because seeking truth is this book's subject, I have chosen perfect truth in Jesus's statement as the basic Bible text for the book.

Reminder: I have decided to use the words *perfect truth* as the basis for this work, reasoning that it can be clearer if we stay with one definition. Again, please note as you read that they are used solely to identify the creative Spirit of Christ's omnipresence as discussed within this book. It is in no way intended to be another name for the deity. My use of the word *truth* in its normal sense is printed in regular lettering.

5
God's Timetable

God's Timing Is Always Right

God gave us time so there would be a time slot for everything that needs to be done. He operates with the limits he puts on it within the scope of eternity (Eccles. 3:15).

"But when the fullness of the time was come, God sent forth his Son" (Gal. 4:4).

The Bible tells us that God's sending a Savior into the world has been planned from the very beginning. And so with perfect timing, the angel Gabriel appeared in Nazareth to tell Mary she'd been chosen to help reset history's clock. She was going to become the virgin mother of a holy child who would save his people. This came to pass in Bethlehem as prophesied. Augustus Caesar had announced a plan earlier that caused Joseph to take Mary along when he went there to register. A signal had already been assigned for a star to send out a birth announcement to gentiles in the east. Earth's tectonic plates had been set to spring beneath the city of Jerusalem thirty-three years from then to shake the temple on a Friday afternoon. A short time later they would move enough in the dark to help roll a stone away from a tomb. By this time, Greek had become the language of the empire so people everywhere could get the message. An efficient system of roads enabled traveling to the outskirts of their civilization. Pax Romana, the peace of Rome, meant you could go anywhere without passports or border checks. Religious freedom under the Romans allowed the gospel to take root and prosper for nearly half a century before the emperor discovered this was not just an ethnic dispute among the Jews.

Throughout history, God's Word tells us "behold, now is the day of Salvation." (2 Cor. 6:2) It is the best of times.

While considering the element of time, we must take into account biblical teachings and the way we normally think, and also what time now means for modern-day science. This is an important area that is rarely mentioned as being an element in our spiritual growth and understanding. The first chapter of Genesis makes it plain: On the fourth day, God installed the sun, moon, and stars to regulate the seasons, days, and years. In Genesis 8:22, he reaffirms the value of time when he promised Noah that as long as earth lasted, there would be seasons to plant and reap, varying seasons and climate. Jesus confirms our understanding of the system when he acknowledges we have daylight to work and nighttime to sleep. No one ever resets a sundial. Yet as scholars studied Einstein's theory of relativity and related subjects, they learned there is another side of time. It is a tool to help measure space. Tape measures, yardsticks, mile markers, and slide rulers are no longer enough. Normally, we use time to direct our activities the way we use length, width, depth, and height. It is useful as we apply our ability to take advantage of opportunities and limited resources in our visible hands-on environment. Right now, while you are reading this, scientists; students; health-care workers, physicians, dentists and their patients; and anyone involved with radiation are dealing with our invisible world. Time has become an important measuring tool never mentioned as such in plain words in the Bible. What else does perfect truth hold that we are yet to learn? "With God, all things are possible" (Mark 10:27).

6
Our Personal Truths

Finding "Our" Truth in Perfect Truth

How is it possible to reconcile millions of individual personalities into one faith?

How is it possible to be one body in the church of Jesus Christ?

In general, people accept that any statement is true whenever it states facts. A great many statements though, especially those that can have more than one interpretation, bring out a chorus of "Yes, but!" The problem is with the word *normally*. A friend went into a deli and asked for an Italian sub. The person behind the counter asked, "What do you want on it?" My friend replied, "Oh, whatever's normal." The clerk replied, "Normal is whatever you want it to be."

The perceived truth of any statement is going to balance between the actual words and the hearer's understanding of normal. To find agreement on the true meaning of any sentence, then, means to agree on the normal common ground of understanding.

There is only one gospel. Does that mean "one size fits all"? Apparently. "For there is none other name under heaven given among men, whereby we must be saved." (Acts 4:12) Now we know that there is disagreement on all kinds of issues among believers and nonbelievers alike, not just in "religion and politics" but in every area of life where people share space. Recognizing these honest differences among the lives of the faithful is of great importance when comparing our differing truths. Our standard is perfect truth.

Where All Truths Are Measured

To adapt from Martin Luther's saying about the world, "finding truth is like a drunk man climbing up onto a horse. He climbs up one side and falls off the other. Then he climbs back up the other side and falls off the first side etc." It's like driving down the highway, weaving from side to side, colliding with others going the opposite way. In daily life, it is even more complicated. Not only do we collide head-on with some but also sideswipe others going our way.

For example, when Jesus says, "I am the Way," who of us can draw the absolutely perfect centerline-of-God's-will teachings to follow on the way? Believers have as many descriptions of how to enter and travel along that way as there are denominations, and all of them have prayerfully sought for reasons to honestly justify their belief. How can they all be "true"? Could it be that God has served each one of us our portion or fair share of perfect truth for "such a time as this"? (Esther 4:14)

Picture perfect truth as an infinite and fine boundary line separating truth and error. As any perceived truth (i.e., statement, belief, supposition, or idea) is brought up to that boundary line in faith, it does not "fall over to the other side of the horse." Instead, teetering in the balance, it is judged and reconciled within himself and by Jesus who is the perfect truth. I see it as somewhat like the refining process that separates the impurities from silver or gold. (Mal. 3:3) He refines the ore of our truth, taking away the dross and bringing pure truth into unity with his perfect truth while leaving the memories with us. He blesses what is right and holds it intact for us with other treasures we are laying up in our relationship with him. Where we are still missing the mark—or "falling over to the other side" (like the man and the horse)—our forgiven flaws stay with us, part of our human Adam's image condition (1 Cor. 15:49), as cited in the familiar Christmas carol, "Adam's likeness now efface, Stamp Thine image in its place" ("Hark! The Herald Angels Sing" stanza 4). His grace continues to help us keep our faith balance as we grow in knowledge. We are ambassadors of this saving message that God was in Christ reconciling the world unto himself, not imputing their trespasses unto them (2 Cor. 5:19).

Picture this: Two Christians study a passage of scripture together. They agree its meaning is important for salvation. But what if they don't agree on how it is to be understood or taught? How is it to be applied to life? Is this passage to be taken literally? Or is it meant to be a figure of speech or a parable? Exactly how important is it as a salvation question? Who taught each of them what they already believe in the first place? Both of these believers are sincere in Christ. Now picture them agreeing in love to prayerfully give it over to God, each believing according to their faith, each believing perfect truth as they are able to receive it. Picture them trusting in Christ alone, God's saving grace. Picture them agreeing to humbly share their faith with one another and those around them. Does not each of them have a corner of the truth? Both of them have only one gospel with Jesus for the Cornerstone (Eph. 2:20). To be sincere in Christ tops the list. (We know the apostle Paul was totally sincere before he was converted, but that wasn't enough; without Christ, he was sincerely wrong.)

7
Truths' Different Reasons

Varying Definitions

The difficulty in finding truth stems from different sources. One is that many people, including scholars, disagree as to the nature of truth depending upon their world outlook, what they hope to find, or their area of interest. For instance, if a tree falls in the forest, does it make a sound if there is no one there or a microphone to hear it? The truth may be judged differently by someone studying the origin of sound waves, a hearing specialist, or a wildlife observer. Is something a truth because it can be tested in a laboratory or by observation? What if the wrong test is used? What if the person announcing the results lies about them? What if something is so obvious that everyone knows it's true, such as, for thousands of years, nearly everyone believed the earth was flat? Some truths are accepted because they seem reasonable. Doubters may claim the wrong reasons are given. The old adage says, "Seeing is believing." That seemed like a reasonable truth since the very beginning, but small children need to be taught that is not true. The subject of this book is based on the kind of truth that comes under a belief in God that cannot be tested by any known methods and is accepted solely by faith.

A Faith Definition

Perfect truth is the superlative standard for all truths. Every worldly truth falls short since our own perfection can never be complete. As believers in faith, we hold our human understanding and doctrines up against Christ's perfect truth. He validates our truth as we are able to grasp it. Errors, misconceptions, and sometimes doubts within our own idea of truth may still linger. Adam's image is still stamped upon us as we walk toward perfect truth. So here is an important question: As long as I am on this side of eternity, how can I claim that the way I practice my personal faith is the only way to follow Christ? Or how can I say that your way, as one of his believers, is wrong?

Gospel truth is accepted by faith. The truths of the Bible give us knowledge, and we believe them because they come from the words God gives us. We can tell others what Christ has done for us. Believers delight in pointing out ways that God's truth is at work in the lives of others. But spiritual truth is hard to prove via bar graphs and test-tube experiments. The truths we hold, mixed in with the limits of our individual traits, learning, and experience, can never be identically the same in two different minds. Yes, perfect truth alone can bring all together in Christ.

Truth Is the Living Boundary in the Gap between True and False / Good and Evil

An illustration: Compare perfect truth with a magnet for iron (Ezek. 22:20). All iron, including that which is mixed with impurities, is drawn toward a magnet. All the impure dross tends to ignore the magnet and feels no sense of attraction. Picture this as an example of Christian experience. Christ draws us to himself. As we receive and join him, he attracts and holds us to himself as the magnet holds the iron. He removes the dross—now sins forgiven—which is rejected and forgotten.

Beyond the illustration: We bring to Jesus a complicated mixture. Even after we are saved and until the end of our days, we are subject to the weaknesses and temptations that so easily beset the flesh. As we live and move and have our being within the boundaries of his Grace, though, we do not worry. Those faults need not control our future. As we truly confess, he is faithful to forgive and cleanse (1 John 1:9). He will not judge us by counting and balancing our actions.

Profound Truth for All Age Groups

Some believers shy away from using the words *story* or *storytelling* in connection with the Bible because they suggest fiction, which I do understand. The words are used here though in a generic sense to join them directly with a present-day phenomenon. If we seek perfect truth in our modern world, we need a theology that speaks to every phase of our civilization. And one of the huge areas dominated by electronic devices today is storytelling. I mean the unreal world of the entertainment industry, which exists in never-never land.

Before alphabets, hieroglyphics, or drawings on cave walls existed, storytelling was the only way to remember history. Besides history, it also serves as a device to help listeners and readers remember a lesson or, sometimes, just to grasp the point of a specific truth. We are familiar with the way Jesus uses this method by making up unforgettable parables that contain valuable gems of truth. He could picture an anxious woman who misplaced a silver coin and ransacked the house until she found it (Luke 15:8–10). He could describe two men building houses, one of them in too big a hurry to do the job right (Matt. 7:24–27). He could call up a mental picture of a hypocrite actually swallowing a camel, hump and all, without realizing what he was doing (Matt. 23:24). As children, we were taught that these parables are "earthly stories with heavenly meanings." But even though parables convey truth in both Old and New Testament settings, there does not seem to be anywhere in the Bible that they, or any other passage for that matter, are recorded simply for the entertainment value. Reading the Bible can certainly give one a sense of peace and comfort or a spirit of satisfaction and joy. Individual passages definitely relate to certain situations. It is written, though, in its entirety as God's Word recording the history of salvation through Jesus Christ from Genesis to Revelation.

8
The Idea of Fairness

A Spirit of Fairness—a Root
of Many Kinds of Evil

A very important quality of perfect truth operating in personal relationships is "Is that fair?" This is a legitimate question. It agrees with our principle that we should love one another. On the upside, it means we don't want to cheat anyone. "I don't want what isn't rightfully mine. We all go by the same rules." In the area under the surface, especially where there is no interest in what Jesus says, "If it's fair, I better get my share," here is where perfect truth seeks to balance God's will. This attitude is so important when it involves large numbers of people that I think it deserves treatment beyond the scope of this book. It is a root cause of war, and here it is in a nutshell: From infancy, I have wanted things to go my way. As an adult, I work at this constantly. It's who I am. I expect society to respect that right and also expect the government to protect it. It's my due. When the heads of government negotiate, they are there to make deals in the collective interests of their respective nations. That means me. Then after everyone goes home, those whose interests were met are pleased. Those who feel they didn't get their fair share go home and begin to talk about getting even. Perhaps you may want to pursue the subject yourself especially if you have connections with children and youth. It may be as important as some other subjects in trying to close up communication gaps.

In the church: One of the places we expect fairness is in the church. As believers, we know the two greatest commandments are to "love the Lord thy God with all thy heart, with all thy soul, with all thy mind, and with all thy strength" and "thou shalt love thy neighbor as thyself" (Mark 12:30–31). In the church's very early days, fairness became an issue. This was in the unfair distribution of food for their widows. The apostles decided that deacons should be selected to make sure they all got their share (Acts 6:14). Then, as followers of the Way branched out into Gentile territory, conflicts arose over the rite of circumcision (Acts 15:1–33). Some said, "If we must be circumcised, why shouldn't this apply to everybody else that becomes a follower of Jesus?" So after a council meeting where apostles, leaders of the home congregation in Jerusalem, along with Paul and other foreign missioners met, the church made a decision. They agreed to refer to the verse or verses that would have instructions that would be fair to all. This meeting is a model for churches in every generation. My hunch is that not every brother went home really happy, but the believers went out and turned the world upside down. Perfect truth prevailed through the guidance of the Holy Spirit to unify the church and carry on the Great Commission.

Life Is Not Fair, but God Is Good

The church is one place where we should expect fair play even if we do not always agree on certain issues. Whether or not something is fair is really intangible. You can't weigh or measure it; it must be perceived. If a brother or sister feels they are losing something, perhaps because decisions are about something material or changing something, there can be a sense of unfairness. This is important in all church business. Lots of decisions deal with doctrines, church practices, and programs that don't seem to have anything to do with fairness. Yet they all have to do with our spirits/emotions and how we feel about things. Everything has to do with how fairly we are treating Jesus. Sometimes I think we would be more sensitive to perfect truth in our midst if we were more alert to our spiritual side. The Bible speaks in terms of a spirit of knowledge, spirit of meekness, judgment, jealousy, grace, truth, slumber, glory of God. Modern language has erased all awareness of how spiritual we really are and has replaced spirituality with the word *emotion*. The entertainment and food industries have been capitalizing on this for decades with their manufactured spiritual comfort foods.

Churches make decisions in various ways depending on how they are organized. No matter how business is done, there are sometimes those who feel it was not fair. Some churches are quite democratic, and decisions are made by the members. Some get their directions through levels of authority. Some are governed by an individual or group of individuals at the top. Some officials are elected, some appointed. Some have rigid rules that have been passed down through generations. Some decide things on their own as needed. If you are a believer, you should fit somewhere in here. With all these many differences, though, we are all members of the body of Christ and subject to him as head of the body and final authority.

I was told this story by a deacon from a fairly democratic church. One day, he asked a fellow worker in the steel mill, "How can you accept that what the pope tells you is really right or wrong? He's only a man and nobody is perfect." The answer was to this effect: "It doesn't mean he's perfect and can't be wrong. It's just that we accept that somebody has to be an umpire. With all the differing opinions there are out there, someone has to agree on the rules so we can play the game." I'm not sure that's how it really is, but it is one person's perspective.

How Precious Is Truth?

Perhaps one of the problems we have with ideas of what is really true or fair is affected by the social climate of our own society.

What we consider fairness in the church reflects also on how our lives as citizens are bundled up with believers and unbelievers alike. There are over three hundred million souls in the United States, and everyone is to be treated with equal justice under the law. When any law is enacted, the Supreme Court has the job of making sure it is in line with the constitution. Whether the court decides for or against that particular law, note one thing: There are nine judges. There has to be an odd number on the bench to make sure of a fair decision. One human being can make a decision for three hundred million others. I use this as an illustration to point out how precious truth and right are to all of us and hoping to get more men, women, and youth to recognize the will of God acting out in everything that happens. How many of those three hundred million are really sheep without a shepherd? Perfect truth resides within the body, mind, and soul of everyone, and they do have a place in God's plan even though it is a fact that modern society in all age groups is being enticed to submit more and more of our decisions into instructions from man-made objects. Look at this example from the world of sports.

For well over a century, baseball games have relied on imperfect umpires to call balls and strikes and to decide if runners are safe or out. Since both sides in a contest have agreed, the game is played fairly as the umpire decides the truth for every pitch thrown. Likewise, for many years, football games have relied upon referees to make sure the rules of the game are obeyed and to judge the progress or losses of both teams. Because of our widespread dependence upon electronic decisions, though, umpires and referees are no longer deemed adequate to make judgments on a game played by professional human beings. So much is at stake that truth must be clear without any doubt. If a baseball manager protests a baserunner's being called "out" by the umpire, the umpire then appeals to a higher authority who has it recorded on television. After the authority relays back the electronic device's version of the "truth," the final decision is announced. In a similar way, a football coach may protest the referee's calling a play out-of-bounds; he disagrees with the ruling that the player's foot was outside the white line. In the same kind of routine, the referee appeals to a higher authority to make a decision based on electronic evidence. I can imagine a time, not too far away, when there is a disputed play, but it won't delay the game as much. Delays are extremely important to the sports industry, of course, since they know time is money. The referee says, "Will the fans please have a moment of silence while I get another opinion?" As a reverent hush falls over the crowd, he says, "Alexa, was the runner's foot inside or outside the line?"

It's Always Personal

One of the problems with discerning perfect truth is expressed very well in traditional sculptures or pictures of Lady Justice. The woman is holding balance scales in her hand, which means justice will be administered equally to everyone. There will be no partiality toward anybody whether rich or poor, friend or enemy, neighbor or stranger; there will be total fairness for everyone involved. The statue of blind justice—or at least the principle involved—is a figure in courthouses and law schools everywhere. Also, the original sculptor wisely included one other truth: Lady Justice herself will not tell you when the scales are perfectly balanced; she is blindfolded. You must make that decision for yourself.

Electronic methods of measuring and testing for truth and accuracy are all around us. In all the traditional crafts, trades, industries, and laboratories, traditional tools of weighing and measuring have become relics. Although new ways offer efficiency and better results for us in many situations, this has brought us around to where we incorrectly assume that mankind's inventions are flawless and can eventually solve all our problems.

9
Separation of Church and Science

Holding to Established Doctrine

The church is at a disadvantage today because traditional theologies seem to be losing relevance as a result of not having kept pace with all the advances of the scientific world. I believe that our teachings are grounded in a biblical worldview of a world that no longer exists. It may not be so much that people have simply turned their backs on God's Word. I believe that it's my generation that has not learned how to communicate God's Word in our society's developing new language. We are lagging behind this new language in the world of our children in the twenty-first century.

For over a thousand years, the church had sole authority to say what was true or false not only in religious matters but also in government, in business, and in the world of nature.

Then, along came men like Copernicus and Galileo with ideas new to the religious domain. Although their ideas had some acceptance in the church, they finally were rejected, along with threats of excommunication. Over the years, however, following more research and discovery and after the Reformation's upheaval died down, a truce developed.

But over a period of time, the church gradually shifted from outright rejection of new ideas to a suspicious acceptance as new knowledge proved to be accurate in more ways. Science gradually earned a legitimate place in the eyes of the church. In time, believers could feel free to enter the field of scientific research. From now on, the church would devote more of its attention to matters of faith and the Bible.

In the search for perfect truth, there would always be a degree of tension between the traditional biblical thinking and newly discovered truths. (There will be new truths announced as long as there are inventors, dreamers, and innovators.) The church still claimed the authority to challenge anything immoral or that otherwise went against biblical truths. At the same time, she would be aware of progress and keep one eye on what scientists were doing. Science would investigate things of the world that we can see, hear, smell, taste, and touch. Also, it became easier now for the church to follow what was happening because we actually had active members of the church working firsthand in the search for new information. They also became involved with new inventions. They were able to bring their knowledge and experience along with them into our church worship, Sunday school classes, and Bible studies. Our traditional biblical overview would provide standards to measure the suitability of new pronouncements.

Peaceful Neighbors

This process worked quite well for the church. On the same level in the twenty-first century, we need to engage the next generations in serious conversation of how God in their "work-a-day" world ties in with their worship experience. Perhaps you can look around in your own faith community to see how this may be a place to begin crossing some gaps. A hundred years ago, one benefit was that now there was plenty of time and energy to devote to examining doctrines, checking out current theological movements, developing missions. It also provided opportunities for healing some of the wounds that occurred during the civil war era. This system worked fairly well for generations. When scientists announced some new "truth" that was questionable, the church turned to the Bible and traditional beliefs to wrestle with the validity of the subject. This did not mean there would always be agreement among believers. My parents remembered the days when there was debate about the morals of driving an automobile. Also, many in the church were active in the field of research and understood the subject at hand. This workable arrangement was essentially disrupted at the end of World War II with the detonation of two atomic bombs in Japan. *A downside of this looking inwardly as stewards of all that's religious, sensing that science was not really a threat, was a diminishing awareness of the holiness of all creation.* While the gods of this world stayed awake, the cautious spirit of our ancestors had drifted off while the gods hid in plain sight.

In 1945, the Atomic Age Exploded on the Scene—Science Turned a Corner That Would Change the Whole World, and the Church Was Not Ready!

Blown away

Before the arrival of the Atomic Age, one of the basic truths in our science books was that matter can neither be created nor destroyed. This "truth" disappeared when successful atomic bomb explosions proved to the world that matter could be separated into its subatomic parts. At that time, since it was a little-known subject and probably never discussed much in high school classrooms, some teachers instructed students just to change the word *matter* in their textbooks to *energy*. I doubt if the teachers understood a whole lot more about it themselves. I remember that same fall of 1945, our ninth-grade science teacher described to us what this was all about by drawing diagrams on the blackboard. We had already learned that everything is actually composed of molecules which were held together by atoms which were held together by other tiny little substances which were way beyond our comprehension. She tried to show how, when the powerful force that held them all together was released, it turned into energy that could be harnessed for industrial use. Also, there were hopes that this newly found source of power would be a valuable source of energy able to drive steamships across the ocean and generate power for industry.

Beyond that, I don't think most people had the slightest idea of the great change this would bring into our lives through other ways of using this new knowledge. Outside of those involved in nuclear research or whoever studied it, I doubt if there were more than a handful of men and women who had the faintest idea of what all this meant for our familiar civilization. Of course, those in the scientific field for a long time, who understood what this was all about, knew that it was more than bomb explosions. They had an eye to the future and hopes for many new things. But I doubt if back then anyone really understood the powerful effects it would have on actually changing civilization as we knew it. The main things that we understood at that time were that besides a tremendous explosion, it also produced a radioactive poison. That was something else to generate fear. No one questioned what this might mean for our foundation theologies. I believe that shock and awe drew our attention away from anything besides the pure violence and destruction that we witnessed. We had to remember, God was still in charge of everything. He was still at work in the world, and what we needed to do was continue to walk in the many trustworthy time-tested spiritual paths we learned over the centuries.

Partnerships of research and development arose to explore new areas of our environment and learned how to develop tools that enabled us to do things that were impossible to do before. It was generally accepted that humans now had access to a power that could destroy the world as we know it, but even with this potential threat of disaster, there was no indication that splitting the atom would separate the direction the world would travel from the pathway of familiar religious beliefs. Two thousand years ago, as the New Testament was being written, there were men who believed in the existence of atoms. Even a mustard seed, as tiny as it was, could be ground into smaller pieces until they were so small that they would be invisible. The tiniest bits that finally could be cut no smaller would be atoms. Actually, there were brilliant thinkers of early antiquity who came up with theories of atomism, but the church mostly shied away from the subject; it had too many connections to the pagan world and human philosophies.

What They Couldn't Know

From the beginning, the church relied on its only source of information—the Bible. How could anyone add anything better to the wisdom of the wisest man who ever lived? The Bible tells us that King Solomon was wiser than any other man (1 Kings 4:31). He spoke over three thousand proverbs, and his songs were 1,005. He taught about animals, reptiles, birds, and fish. He understood about plant life from the cedar tree to the little hyssop growing out of a crack in the wall. The record indicates that he was aware of earth science and geography. He obviously knew a thing or two about horse-trading and other business. He had a real grasp of politics. The Bible says, "And God gave Solomon wisdom and understanding exceedingly much, and largeness of heart, even as the sand that is on the seashore" (1 Kings 4:29). But it never mentions the limit of his head knowledge on any subject. His gifts of wisdom, understanding, and insights would make him a valuable asset to a modern think tank. Looking back at the record, though, with what we know today, it may be safe to say that he could have taught his factual scientific knowledge to a bright junior high student in two semesters. Wisdom is another subject, which begins with a healthy reverence for the Lord's providence and can take a lifetime to acquire. Perfect truth has it all.

It turns out, however, as scholars learned how to trust the laws and predict their behavior through observation and experiments, the door opened to modern research and development. New tools were invented to look into a formerly hidden world of truths.

Ancient scholars had no ability to test their atomic theories, of course, but they could imagine it. By the twentieth century, so much had been learned about atoms that thinkers like Albert Einstein, and others in the field, had theories about how to separate atoms into their smaller parts. For many years, it was accepted that our school desks appeared to be solid wood, but they were not. It was general knowledge that water is composed of hydrogen and oxygen, table salt is sodium and chloride. Everything is a whirling mass of molecules and their atoms. They never actually touch each other but are in a tightly knit relationship within their own spaces. Without modern microscopes or other instruments, those ancient scholars had no clue as to the existence of a subatomic world with all kinds of possibilities and potential. As it turns out, the discovery of that hidden world, beyond our range of sight, hearing, smell, taste, and touch, was almost like finding another planet. It was different from any other discovery in history. Whenever the Americas were discovered, it was not long before missionaries came along with explorers to convert the souls that they had found here. But when crossing the frontier into the subatomic world, there was no hint that we would be facing the spiritual and moral questions that face us today. We did not realize that science had thrown us a curve that traveled into a new world with a new language. Nobody even warned us to swing at the ball.

Huge challenges are brought to us by developments in artificial intelligence, gene-splicing, cloning, and other things that were unheard of before 1950. The questions raised by progress in these three areas alone do not appear to have very clear answers in any church teachings with which I am familiar. In fact, at the present time, when there is a serious debate about nudity on social media, the industry is looking for ways to involve artificial intelligence to help make the decision!

Clues to Our Missing the Signals

I think several reasons why atomic research, the invention of computers, and other research in the electronic world in general never came under serious religious discussion is because the atomic bomb blew us out of the science laboratory. The shock and awe of such mass destruction was gut-wrenching in itself. Atomic energy just seemed like a more efficient way to cause devastation. I think another more subtle but just as important factor is that, as time went by, scientific research and discovery had proved their value. The church basically trusted the field of science. The suspicions of earlier centuries were long gone, and many men and women in the modern science classrooms were Christian. By the time the transistor made its appearance in the late 1940s, the development of which made computers possible, the church never noticed. Research and development were becoming more important in altering life as we knew it, but they were no longer on our radar.

A key incentive for researchers in any field is that their faith and hope in tried-and-true methods will produce certain results. They also are prepared for surprises and learn to adjust to new data. Past experience with inventions and experiences in many fields means that it will work in the future. Science has discovered amazing things and, by now, has accomplished what would have been miracles in years gone by. You and I probably enjoy our life and health and maybe even the fact that we are alive thanks to the efforts of unknown scientists. There is one thing in all progress, though, that has always been interesting to me: Nearly everything has been accomplished while working with a flawed system of numbers. Spaceships fly around the universe. Women and men survive in space capsules.

A rocket can land on an asteroid, pick up samples, and fly back toward earth. And this all happens despite one deficiency in the process: the math. Mathematics is sometimes called the *exact science*. Civilization has depended on it for years. The fly in the ointment is in the dictionary definition of the word *pi*. Pi is the symbolic designation of the circumference of a circle to its diameter. It defines it as *about* 3.1416. About. We can add all the zeroes in the universe, but that's as close as anybody can get. The perfection is in perfect truth. Practical researchers never even stop to think of this as a limitation though. They make progress using what they already know: it works. Surely, this can be a lesson for our faith journey. All that anyone can do is to faithfully think and act with the gifts and talents the Holy Spirit has granted to each one; it works. All the believers' flaws and shortcomings are made perfect because our perfection is in Christ.

If It's Cut and Dried, Something Died

Another sign of promise from our scientific community: even with all their modern accomplishments, they do acknowledge they hope to do better someday. Science never lays claim to being perfect or having all the answers. It expects progress, hardly perfection. It is well to keep in mind that multitudes of these women and men—teachers, students, employees—are people of faith. The Bible does instruct everyone, including them, not to be thrown off track by dead-end goals and principles of this world (Col. 2:9). The world's wisdom is foolishness (1 Cor. 1:20). Frequently, when science and faith occur in the same conversation, there are hints of spiritual inequality.

That is one reason there is a discipline called "the philosophy of mathematics." Mathematicians are never satisfied with what has already been done but are seeking also for what it really means for life and the universe in general. All things are possible with God. One time in math class, the professor was explaining a particular point to us, and said, "I want to be sure you understand this, before you fall into the hands of those corrupt logicians." On one occasion, I met him walking across campus and asked, "Is our system of numbers something that men invented, or was it in the universe, and they discovered it?" He replied, "You'll have to ask that question in philosophy class." Another time he said, "If anyone asks you, 'How much is two plus two?' tell them, 'As far as we know now it's four.'"

Over the years, the main thing I recall when discussing the ways of science was that we would remind ourselves, "Science says, 'I think I can do this.' The church asks the question, 'I wonder if you ought to?'" Then we left them to figure out the answer themselves.

One thing, though, did not change; the apostle Paul wrote, "The god of this world hath blinded the minds of them which believe not" (2 Cor. 4:4). Nothing has changed. Jesus said, "Lift up your eyes and look on the fields. For they are white already to harvest" (John 4:35). To this day, the prince of darkness is still leading whole generations of his flock away from the Light.

10
Changing Times

Changing Surroundings

Another compelling reason for the church taking its eyes off the new branches of science was the ending of World War II itself. The Christian community had many tasks ahead in the immediate future. The country was turning back to a civilian economy with millions of returning veterans and wartime workers needing jobs. There were new families on the horizon to be established, homes to be built. While the church was involved with all this on one hand, there also was an awareness of the needs of devastated millions in Europe who had survived seven years of war. Programs were developed for ways to provide material and spiritual aid to help relieve their suffering. By 1950, the church was experiencing a growth in "church building" that accompanied a revival. This was evidence that the wisdom of our tried and true doctrines had well prepared us for developing the church and for the good results in the life of the congregation. But meanwhile, the enthusiastic world of science had gone around a corner and down a rabbit hole to explore and work in this new world hidden from our sight. I believe one irony is that during the last seventy years, thousands of these women and men, especially in the health field, have been believers. They come to worship, Sunday school, and Bible studies with us, yet none of us could realize that their progress and their new developments would help lead to the present mass confusion throughout our modern world. This still occurs today. Believers, seeking to defend the faith, faithfully keep to the path without seeing that the lost sheep in front of us out in the world have turned off onto a new route.

Another drawback to our traditional theologies is that they have not kept up with the developments that are actually changing the way people think. The message of perfect truth is still proclaimed through faith statements and doctrines that the church tested and tried over twenty centuries. But that was still in a time when new ideas and inventions came from the minds and experiences of women and men who understood the known laws of our visible world. Society responded to anything new according to their knowledge of a world where everything was visible and could be weighed, measured, or tested in some way. Human beings have not visibly changed. We are still patterned after Adam and Eve with the same potentials for good and bad. The gospel has not changed, and God's providence is still in control. What has changed, though, is the growing power our culture has over us while the culture itself is being swallowed up by the mindless powers of an industrialized economy.

It appears that the force of scientific research has redirected the path of civilization into an area that offers no directives or correctives for the upheaval, uncertainty, and frustration in the world. The only permanent and unchanging thing we have is the Bible which promises Joshua "the Lord thy God is with thee withersoever thou goest" (Josh. 1:9). James tells us, "Draw nigh to God, and he will draw nigh to you. Resist the devil, and he will flee from you" (James 4:7–8). We need prayer for Holy Spirit guidance through the difficulties and unseen pitfalls all around.

Computers Invade the Scene

The ability of computers to think, calculating at high speeds, makes them an important part of our lives and has led to many modern-day blessings. Some of us appreciate them most when they lead to improvements in our health care. However, their ability to develop new ways to do things to the mind and body and the ability to make unhuman decisions are raising some red flags. Whenever a person's conscience doesn't feel right about something that the computer says is the best choice, which one will win out? Over time, how is this affecting the commonly accepted notions of society, including believers, about what is right and wrong and how we should act? The ethics of artificial intelligence is being studied in colleges and at special conferences. Among those grappling with these developments is a cross section that includes Christians, skeptics, undecided and nonbelievers. Surely, the believers among them deserve all the help they can get from their church.

True Wisdom

Intelligence, much like truth, is a self-evident faculty or power in human beings that needs no explanation. It's just there in our brain's computer as a fact of life. We can discuss it, describe it, and decide how to handle it, but that doesn't change it. The Bible never really defines intelligence but devotes itself to teaching us how to use it. Wisdom is a related subject and is needed to nourish and regulate our use of intelligence. The entire scriptures are bathed in God's wisdom and often make reference to it especially in Proverbs. A keynote text says, "The fear of the Lord is the beginning of wisdom; and the knowledge of the holy is understanding" (Prov. 9:10–11). Portions of chapters 3, 4, 8, and 9 describe how wisdom thinks and acts in ordinary life. Jesus tells us that wisdom is revealed by its results (Matt. 11:35). Paul's writing about it offers a pitiful comparison between our wisdom and God's. "Because the foolishness of God is wiser than men" (1 Cor. 1:25). Current events, blindly following promises from the ruler of this world, show us once again that self-serving human wisdom has no real answers. The only way to open up intelligence to God's wisdom is through the foolishness of preaching the gospel (1 Cor. 3:21). As it happens, a humanly devised computer is limited solely to the wisdom of whoever programmed it.

The Bible never actually defines what life is either. It has many teachings and live illustrations of how to live and how not to live. It indicates what it is not (Matt. 6:25). What we do know is that when God breathed life into the nostrils of the man created in his own image, Adam became a living soul with intelligence. Then God made him a companion who would be his counterpart in producing children imprinted with their human design. We now see how we have inherited the gift of intelligent life along with its connection to the living chain that unites us with God's original creation. We also have assurance of the great truth that Jesus Christ is the same yesterday, and today, and forever (Heb. 13:8).

JOHN E. EASH

The Silver Lining

No matter how dismal the spiritual condition of the world looks, Peter reminds us that the prophets said this would happen. Looking back over history and the ups and downs of the church, this occurs repeatedly. Scoffers choose to not believe and to ignore what happened in Noah's time. Judgment is coming. The day of the Lord will come as a thief in the night. Jesus said his return could be at midnight or morning (Mark 13:35). But here's the bright side: "The Lord is not willing that any should perish but that all should come to repentance." Amid all the lies, hypocrisy, moral filth, and violence going on, the providential will of God within perfect truth is already out there waiting. It's time to show the world that we have a better way. It can be tempting sometimes to adapt to some of the world's ideas and adjust the message to get a better hearing. But Jesus said we are to go into the world with the gospel, and "lo, I am with you to the end of the world" (Matt. 28:20).

11
A Modern Challenge

Wheat and Tares Blend

Along with atomic energy, there is another serious challenge to our beliefs and practices that arose shortly after the end of World War II. In fact, it may even be as important as any other biblical problems we try to understand. What happened here was this newcomer, electronics, quietly walked in through our back door right after the war ended. What is the church's biblical understanding of the world of electronics? In fact, we have been caught flatfooted by computers. Small children play with them. They surround us in our homes. They are in our churches, our schools, our homes, on our wrists, and in our pockets. Every congregation and most believers are aware that they have surrounded us with new potential for good and, likewise, for evil. I contend that perfect truth in every electron in every electronic gadget is seeking a balance according to the laws God used in their development. Our responsibility as believers is to discover their legitimate use. Every electronic gadget contains the same perfect truth that holds the universe together, including the book you are reading and the chair under you.

JOHN E. EASH

Faith Mixed in the Soil

Any study of American history soon shows the influence the Bible and spiritual values had upon public policy at all levels of government, in private institutions, and throughout much of society. The main roots of culture, especially among immigrants who came for religious freedom, were grounded in the Bible and their particular religious teaching as well as godly values and traditions they grew up with in their homelands. As the new nation was formed, there was no doubt that the family of faith was going to be an important part of these new beginnings. For this reason, freedom of religion was included in the Constitution's Bill of Rights to make sure the government could not take sides with any particular group. A look at modern history, though, from mid-twentieth century until now will show hardly any reference to the importance these ideas had for many years. In fact, today, there are probably few that are aware of them. I believe this recent history began with the post-World War II era. As the millennial generation takes over management of business and government, around the world, leadership will be largely in the hands of men and women the church does not know.

A vague national awareness of God stays alive by national leaders referring to the Founding Fathers and our singing "God Bless America" at public gatherings. This is lingering fruit produced from roots planted by our forebears. The world certainly has a knowledge that there is a God who has something to do with a baby Jesus and Easter. That may be thanks to the Christmas gift industry and television specials as much as to the church.

"I Am the Bread of Life" (John 6:35)

Meanwhile, there is a hidden unidentified hunger in America; the hunger for God that everyone has inside them from birth. In the city of Athens, Paul says, "He giveth to all life and breath; and hath made of one blood all nations of men that they should seek the Lord, though he be not far from every one of us, we are the offspring of God" (Acts 17:25–29). He came to redeem us, his sons and daughters, through the salvation of Jesus Christ, his son. Four centuries later, Augustine of Hippo writes, "You have made us for yourself, O Lord, and our heart is restless until it rests in you." We often simply call it a hole in the heart that only God can fill with the Holy Spirit. From earliest times, the world, the devil, and our flesh conspire to stifle this heart-hunger with the things of this world. For twenty centuries, we effectively point out, in plain language, that the search for money, physical pleasures, and selfish pride is contrary to what God really has in store. We name the sins and identify the lies of false gods. We warn our youth to avoid the obvious pitfalls because they can see the results of sin. Then, the unholy trinity puts on a new false face, slips in through an unseen door, and creates an electronic environment. Now, seven decades later, we are seeing the result of the same old sins in the same old way, but we can't see how to head it off because of the way it works. The Bible makes it clear what always works for the church: carry out the Great Commission. Translate the Word into the language of those millions now feeding on lies in the presence of perfect truth. The Ten Commandments are still in the Bible. We still preach conversion, confession, and repentance for sin, and—as the old hymn says—"The Way of the Cross Leads Home." The clamor of the world's gods is drowning us out.

12
New Discoveries, New Uncertainties

Illustration of Main Reason for the Book

The prize is still before us

Regardless of how many denominations, independent groups, or congregations are in the world today, all are spiritually united in the body of Christ, his church. Even though we differ in some ways, all are bound together through our faith in basic truths. A partial list would include the incarnation of Jesus Christ and his finished work as Savior and Lord, his message of salvation, his death and resurrection. He is the Way, the Truth, and the Life. God gave the Holy Spirit to help us live as faithful followers day by day and take his gospel message out into a world of sin. There will always be resistance to our mission from the rulers, authorities, and powers of this dark world (Eph. 6:12). Sometimes, this satanic opposition will be in the form of widespread violence as in the days of Emperor Nero or localized as in certain areas of the world now. Today, this resistance works to lead their flocks away from the cross and tomb with wholesale messages of the wonders of this age. For many, death is perceived as a sliding door opening into heaven the way the door opens automatically when you enter a supermarket. Millions are unaware that Jesus said, "But fear not them which kill the body but are unable to kill the soul; but rather fear him which is able to destroy both body and soul in hell" (Matt. 10:28).

All the churches I am familiar with look to the Bible, God's Word in print, for instruction and information pertaining to our faith. Our differing teachings and practices stem from the way our forebears handed down their truths to us and how present-day readers have defined the right responses to basic beliefs. My understanding, though, and the point of this whole book is that variations in doctrine and practices and how we have arrived at them should never detract from our common assignment to go into "the world" with the gospel message. In fact, I believe Paul's message in 1 Corinthians 1:10–13 has somewhat of a bearing on this topic. Christ is not divided.

The primary thrust of this writing is to encourage the search for God's perfect truth in every facet of modern culture, both visible and unseen. Perfect truth will be found as the Bible shows us how it is moving God's will through history toward its final consummation. God offers salvation to every generation in a lost world through his gospel. One of the difficult ministries facing the church today is how to bring this message to generations raised to know a lot about computers and almost nothing about the Bible.

What's in a Name?

Therefore, I want to call our attention to artificial intelligence as important in all this because it produces so much of what we accept as truth today. Since searching for truth in everything includes artificial intelligence as part of the subject, it may be used at times as a tool to examine itself. Because computers were nonexistent back then, it is hard sometimes to see a direct connection with parables and other teachings of Jesus; neither is there much in scripture that seems interested in anything like artificial thinking. As a result, with the way we unthinkingly allow it to influence lifestyles, our Bible studies and Sunday school classes may find artificial intelligence to be extremely difficult to discuss.

A comparison: there is no such thing as an artificial flavor; if something tastes like strawberries, it tastes like real strawberries. If it tastes like vanilla, it is true vanilla flavor. When a label says "artificial flavor," it simply means the flavor is produced by a chemical reaction within artificial ingredients. The same thing applies to any food product containing "imitation flavor"; the flavor is natural but comes from a humanly concocted mixture. Any variations in the quality of flavor depend upon whatever the manufacturer thought would work the best. Food products that contain artificial flavors are made to mimic the natural flavors as nearly as possible. If they succeed, you can't tell the difference. The way they are made shares some similarities to artificial intelligence. As our Creator ascribes intelligence to children from the beginning, so does the computer designer put intelligence into his handiwork. Its performance is intended to imitate human intelligence. I recall whenever computers first began to appear in our daily experience, we were given the reminder "garbage in, garbage out."

The use of artificial intelligence in modern life is so prevalent that it is hard to tell how much effect it has on our lives. Developed as a way to benefit life, it has brought many improvements to industry, business methods, health care practices, education, and the way we conduct our daily routines. Because of all the good things that happen and its positive expectations, it would be wrong to criticize it just for being what it is. Since perfect truth is totally involved, it is necessary to look at it from the Bible's viewpoint to see where it's headed. Every thought in every element of the computer contains the perfect truth inherent in every created element. Artificial intelligence in the hands of believers with God's will intended has all the potential to produce good things for humanity as the Holy Spirit guides. In the hands of unbelievers, it is wide open to the evil ambitions of the god of this world. Practical experience tells us that anything a woman or man invents is theirs to use as they see fit. Inventors have no moral obligation to cater to their brainchild. Isaiah uses tools, such as axes and saws, as examples of this principle (Isa. 10:15).

Should We Be in the Know?

Artificial intelligence (AI) was born in the scientific world of post-1945 and is a product of recent developments. There seems to be no limits to its possibilities. The designers of AI and those who have access to it, many of whom are believers, are limited to the normal ability to reason and to learn. The question is, When AI is brought into play, who is responsible for the results? The designer, programmer, manufacturer, or the person using it? Other questions are as follows: Does the person responsible for the programming transfer the ability to make decisions that would be moral or immoral if carried out by a human? If someone is found to be responsible, then whose standard of morality should apply? Will it make any difference if they are believers or not?

As mentioned elsewhere, the ethics of AI has been a subject of study in higher education and in conferences for some time. I feel quite sure the legal industry is involved with these concerns. In the meantime, the news of our interest as a concern of the church has been an earsplitting silence. Should not this be part of our burden in reaching out to the younger generations?

As children of earthly parents, everyone has a life given by God. Believers have the promise of a new life as children of God but not a natural descent (John 1:12–13). They have a Savior who died that he might give them a new heart. This means looking forward to an eternity with God and all the saints who have gone before. The computer, made with human hands, is a lifeless object. We need spiritual direction now for our existence in a world of robots that can suffer from viruses of their own. As you and I think about all this, it is very important to keep in mind how different age groups relate to these realities.

One of the areas theologians have worked with for centuries is how to define the unseen elements of body, soul, mind, and spirit and their relationship with God. Where do they separate, and how do they interact? If we are the temple of God, where does he reside? Which areas are subject to the desires of the flesh, and how do I control them? Where is our receiver that listens for the voice of God? We benefit from the insights scholars give us from their studies of scripture on these topics. Modern technology adds to our knowledge of the brain and how it handles the information we give it. Now discussions of religion and our faith include the results of this research. Different areas of the brain have different jobs. How do our non-material spiritual elements make connections as body and soul cooperate? There are terms such as the self, ego, id, superego that are to help us grasp how we respond to our thoughts and experiences. As we try to reach today's generations, we need to have some idea of how all these ideas fit together in our own modern minds. It can help our understanding of the Bible as well if we consider that all of our new words apply to the behaviors of every human being mentioned in the Bible. Proverbs, Ecclesiastes, and Job offer a wealth of practical counseling on how one's soul can struggle. Certainly, Solomon has understanding in these areas. At the end of the day, it adds up to the goals of perfect truth-seeking balance as we live within God. What we do with the stuff we invent is up to us (Eph. 3:9–13).

Grapes on Thorns, Figs on Thistles

There are differing reasons for all believers to think carefully about the possibilities of AI. One is that computers can be programmed to provide counseling services. They are intended to interact with a client and make helpful suggestions. They are mindless machines. Most likely, there are legitimate interests planning for helpful ways to take advantage of this for people who need help. With all the godless schemes running through humanity, I would venture to guess that there are evil interests already planning how to misuse these new possibilities for their own gain. What if that advertisement for modern twenty-first-century-quality private personal counseling is a front for a cult?

A friend of mine was scheduled for a heart-valve replacement. After the surgeon explained the procedure, my friend asked him how he could do such things in a beating heart. The doctor explained that they would stop his heart for that time and restart it when the operation was over. My friend thought a moment and then said, "Well, all right. But, Doc, just don't let the pilot light go out!" This, we know, would mean the end of his intelligence modeled after the elements contained in our first earthly parents. It stands to reason then that any life issuing from a computer will be an offspring from the artificial ingredients chosen by its designers. Perfect truth is within AI as in all of creation to maintain balance by the functioning of its own natural laws. But if the pilot light goes out in a computer, it stays out.

Long ago, there were arbitrary lists drawn up of deadly sins. They, of course, had the Ten Commandments and other teachings from the Bible. The list was to warn against feelings that easily lead into sin. This was so believers would know how to make right choices. They served their purpose because not only could individuals take heed, but they could also apply to group behaviors. The list I recall is pride, prejudice, gluttony, anger, lust, envy, and sloth. In a world where common knowledge and experiences are in three dimensions, this works fine. The difficulty comes whenever we try to perceive a sinful spirit within a world nobody knew before the twentieth century. How can we define the moral limits of a kind of life invented by human science and designed to make it enter our brains via robots? At present, when we are confronted by anything like this that doesn't feel right, we can only revert to our default settings, which somehow seem inadequate. Commandments about worshipping other gods and making idols have a bearing on the subject, but I feel sure no one is consciously intending to bow down or to serve them (Exod. 20:1–6). As you, the reader, consider this, perhaps you will think of a way to get a hold on this issue.

With all our advances in scientific study, we know that the intelligence God designed is far more complex than anything the Bible writers could even imagine. Whenever the psalmist declares "what is man that thou art mindful of him? For thou hast made him a little lower than the angels, and hast crowned him with glory and honor. Thou hast given him dominion over the works of thy hands," he is lost in wonder at how awesome God really is (Ps. 8:4–6). To spiritually share the presence of God's holiness and then be entrusted with power to rule over all creation is really too much for words. However, even within that ecstatic joy, he has no inkling of the intelligence network sustaining his life and supervising a network of thirty-seven trillion living cells within him.

13
Electronic Media

The Spiritual Influence of Make-Believe

The entertainment industry utilizes a great number of activities and different methods such as television and present-day modern social media, but motion pictures are my main example. Sometimes I use *Hollywood* as a synonym for movies. I do this to keep an awareness of reciprocating perfect truth in every particle of substance and every moment of time, advancing the sovereign will of God. I am confident that he cares about the souls of all who produce and act in movies, as well as patrons who take time to watch.

The only religious thinking I know of that applies in general to entertainment has to do with our personal motives. They are the standard, time-tested questions. Will it involve any immorality in what you are watching or doing? Will it tempt you to think or to do something wrong? Is it a wise use of your time and money? As to Hollywood in particular, are you encouraging and supporting men and women who live immoral lifestyles?

I understand that many years ago, and it may be today as well, there were devout Christians who were opposed to writing fiction. They felt it would be a sin to create imaginary people and give them souls. Back then, there would have been differing opinions on exactly what and where the soul is, the same as opinions vary today. But they were well aware of important spiritual realities. A fictional character communicates by speaking to the mind of the reader. In the reader's mind, events are taking place via imaginary conversations and real mental pictures that produce living thought patterns. Intense emotions can be stirred in different ways that involve mind, soul, and body. Perfect truth is involved everywhere nudging toward balance. The thoughts, words, and behavior of fictional souls in print can definitely influence our lives with their spiritual impact. In our present electronic age, they do it in real sight, real sound, and living color.

Motion pictures were produced with a profit motive knowing that people spend time and money for amusements that stimulate their emotions in some way. The Bible itself says little about emotions or feelings, and whenever it does, it uses the word *spirits*. Beyond the idea of whether a movie was worth the time and money, there was little thought as to how make-believe tales were imprinted in one's brain. Movies, as entertainment, remained a footnote in life's plan and were not all that important. That is now ancient history. Television ushered in a major game changer.

Since television sets appeared on the scene seventy years ago, the furniture has been rearranged in homes the world over. New homes are built with a space already prepared. Around-the-clock sight and sound are a must in modern society; and it worked its way in as entertainment. Souls that existed only on celluloid in neighborhood theaters before could appear right in front of you at the click of a dial. Plus— not only that—real live performers could amuse you just by pretending they were the fictitious souls in other stories. As with any invention, nothing is good or bad in itself; it is how people use it and for what purpose. Television itself became the leader in developing entertainment as a major industry. Television has been very important to the education industry. It plays a big role in many gospel ministries. It can have a downside though.

Where Untruth Meets Inward Truth

Do we really know what the electronic media has been doing to our souls? Millions of people nowadays are unsettled and at odds with others and do not seem to know what they want. Is it because we have lost sight of what is real? How is the god of this world blinding our eyes? The impact of social media has added complications also. You no longer have to just listen to a newscaster's talk. Now you can talk back to the world. And with the cloak of anonymity, you can pretend just as much as anyone else does. Also, seeing cartoon characters on the screen is no longer enough; you can have a more personal relationship. One is encouraged to go to Disneyland or Disney World to see Snow White and Pinocchio and Goofy "in person"; and you might even get fooled there. I was once told by an adult that the real Mickey and Minnie Mouse live in California; the two characters in Florida Disney World are imitations.

In 1950, one's normal circle of friends and acquaintances was limited to family and friends you saw quite often, get in touch with easily, or call on the telephone. Your capacity to communicate with and maintain a relationship with them was fairly constant. Today, social media have widened that circle to however far you want to enlarge your personal space. How well individuals adapt to these changes depends on one's personality and how much time you have available. Beyond just the instant communication process itself, there is the mental effort required to evaluate and process large numbers of instant messages. It would seem that this provides a completely different framework for us to judge what is true or false than in earlier times. Does this fragment our sense of who we are and our life's goal? Much is being said about the confusing times we live in. The Bible tells us that "God is not the author of confusion," which it records in the context of corporate worship (1 Cor. 14:33). The master of confusion, who sets the agenda for the world, seeks to contaminate the relationships we have between ourselves and others no matter where we are.

Beware of All Idols

We really need to find Holy Spirit guidance to work through these issues. It may be that a steady diet of TV programming over generations has overwhelmed our senses to the point that amusement has become a felt need, and they no longer can detect the difference between true and false. It may be that a person's natural ability to adapt to changes has clouded our thoughts in the same way we learned our other habits.

If we consider the belief mentioned earlier that creating images and giving them souls is sinful behavior, what commentary does this make on the casual unthinking way we treat all kinds of fiction in this day and age? The prophet Isaiah warned us long ago as to how silly this can get. He says it's like a woodcarver using a tree he has cut down. He burns part of it in the fire to cook his meal and part of it to keep warm. Then, after he is comfortable, he takes the leftover part, makes it into a god, bows down to it, and prays,

"Deliver me for Thou art my God" (Isa. 44:14–17). Isaiah knows how to tell it like it is.

The church cannot wait for the world to lift itself up. The evil spirits of the age are not heading in that direction. Jesus says, "If the blind lead the blind, shall not both fall into the ditch?" (Matt. 15:14). "If Satan casts out Satan, he is divided against himself; how then shall his kingdom stand?" (Matt. 12:26). He also talks about people who can see but, at the same time, really do not see or understand. Also, there are people who hear with their ears yet do not understand (Matt. 13:15). Nevertheless, his disciples go out and get the job done trusting him, empowered by the Holy Spirit and without a New Testament to carry.

If we use the computer as an illustration, the problem is not just that our culture is offering new apps to download; it is altering the hard drive at the same time. In our parallel realm of evil, it makes it easier to plug in and swallow AI.

If our only problem was just how to react to the evil that is rampant in the entertainment industry and the evils that have spilled into social media, it would be one thing. This is complicated enough in itself. Yet we can respond with the knowledge that sin can take on any form or use any method it chooses. A big challenge is the protection of children, youth, and other innocents. Where are the safeguards? This is not only a concern on the part of believers. There are parents in many levels of society who are worried about the harmful effects of our electronic world. Jesus says, "Suffer the little children to come unto me......for of such is the kingdom of heaven" (Mark 10:14).

There are other perfectly valid reasons, some material, as to why the church did not pick up on the need to seriously examine this invisible new world. One is the total secrecy surrounding atomic research.

Only a handful of insiders were aware of the direction this "new science" was going. When the bombs fell on Hiroshima and Nagasaki, it registered as just one more sad step in the age-old arts of war.

14
What's New and Vice Versa

Unforeseen Changes

We believe Paul when he wrote, "So we fix our eyes not on what is seen, but what is unseen. For what is seen is temporary. What is unseen is eternal" (2 Cor. 4:18). Another text is from Hebrew 11:3, "By faith, we understand that the universe was formed at God's command, so that what is seen was not made out of what was visible." It was not made out of any combination of atoms and molecules or anything else imaginable.

One of the places of change in recent years is the way we think. Another is the way we have had to respond to new devices that resemble nothing ever seen before. A lot of research has been going into how television and other electronic devices influence the arrangements of brain cells and how they function, especially in children. There is also a fairly recent line of study on how activity within the brain makes connections with spiritual reality. Sometimes called neuro-theology its researchers are examining how they interact. Studying individual minds and faith is not new. For many years, researchers have tried confining God to a laboratory table and studying him the same way as a frog or a squirrel's brain in biology class. Today though, there are studies about the human mind that are bringing in some valuable new information. Something harder to measure in defining spiritual problems, and it is also new, is how people can fully manage their spiritual experience while trying to make sense of a 24-7 industrialized lifestyle. I am referring to a shift in the way we think and have to do things under pressures that seem to have a will of their own. As believers, we strive to live in the world and yet, at the same time, not belong to the world. We believe, "as the truth is in Jesus," we have put aside the old human nature and are renewed in the spirit of our mind (Eph. 4:21–23). We try to shape life to fit our own needs while resisting the world's efforts to print us out in three-dimensional copies of itself. The way you personally deal with these pressures depends on your circumstances and personality and faith. Each of the others around you is responding in his or her own way. Meanwhile, our hope is in the one whose kingdom is not of this world.

Belief Accepts New Knowledge

The Bible indicates in more than one place that God created the heavens and earth out of nothing. In the prescientific world of two thousand years ago, the smallest conceivable thing was the atom. As far as I am aware, men and women did not think of anything smaller. Now, although we know a whole lot more than the ancients did, and our civilization deals with things they never dreamed of, faith still focuses on and moves forward in the direction of eternity beyond this creation. From the beginning, the church literally focused its attention on the things we see and experience mentally and physically and spiritually. Our understandings of how faith applies to any subject are based on time-tested beliefs learned from scripture.

How do all these things fit into God's plan in the light of the Gospel? "For we walk by faith, not by sight" (2 Cor. 5:7). Many of these arise from the writings of Paul and the examples he gives. With no modern knowledge, he knows that there are both the material and the spiritual realms, and he consciously thinks and acts in both of them. He is always aware that what is going on in his physical surroundings is affecting his spiritual future, and the only things permanent are what he can't see. In the same way, when Jesus talks about laying up treasures in heaven, he is saying that present actions are already happening there. There is no evidence, though, that any of the men and women we meet in the Bible ever thought about the existence of another world around them moving at high speed in the material substances around them.

Down through the years, obviously, particular approaches to Christian belief have varied greatly in different areas and among different groups, but one thing all affirm is that Jesus Christ is Lord and Savior. Our marching orders are still the Great Commission. Although beliefs hold firm, actual Christian practices changed, as needed, to meet new knowledge, new obstacles, and new circumstances. Today, however, the church is dealing with issues that the faith of our mothers and fathers could never imagine. Historically, when the church questioned new pronouncements and new discoveries, they relied on their faith that God's Word had all the authority that faith would need to decide the truth. Regardless of results, meaning that sometimes they changed their minds, their faith journey still shows the way through the Word of God to be the way for their generation. As newfound facts led them to accept new truths, their teachings were adjusted accordingly. As we see the need to refresh our traditional views of the natural world, the Bible—given by inspiration of God—gives us a wealth of encouragement (2 Tim. 3:16). Although the New Testament uses the actual words *faith* and *faithfulness*, many times oftener, the Old Testament reveals many examples of faith, doubt, and obedience in the words and actions of its people. In fact, the book of Psalms declares faith on every page. God inspired David who knew only the science of his day to convey a spirit of wonder and awe that matches and often surpasses anything written today.

Perfect Truth in Praise

I lift up Psalm 148 as one passage supporting the need for a completely fresh look at our theologies in the light of recent discoveries. In this chapter, we can almost hear the voices of praise from inanimate objects as well as all creatures that breathe. Read it the first chance you get. Hear the psalmist's exuberant call for praise to the Lord. He begins at the heights of spiritual creation and reaches to the bottom of the sea. He expects praise from every bit of creation and concludes with the praise of all the saints, the people God called to be with him. Could he have praised God any better if he had access to a Hubble Space Telescope? Further, if we think about God's ongoing relationship with the material world, hear what Jesus says on the first Palm Sunday. When he is told to rebuke his disciples for praising him, he says, "I tell you that, if these should hold their peace, the stones would immediately cry out" (Luke 19:40). When the devil tempts him in the wilderness, one of the requests is to turn stones into bread. This hints that Jesus had full awareness of his relationship to inanimate objects, as well as human needs, from the beginning. Perhaps it may be that God wants us to be sure we learn the old melody of creation (a song without music) at the same time he helps you and me discover new lyrics to sing in harmony with the old (a chorus of praise). A spirit of faith and trusting in Jesus gives us the melody with which to sing our words.

The Bible Includes It All

The church didn't pick up on the new direction that science was taking, as it happened outside of our reality and our line of focus. Before that, almost all our natural laws were described in terms we could grasp because they operated within the visible world, and they could be tested. For example, the laws of water displacement, how electricity works, the functions of mathematics, Newton's laws of motion, the law of gravity, etc. were traditional school subjects. I remember the day we learned the Pythagorean theorem in algebra class. That evening I proudly explained it to my father who grew up on a farm and had only an eighth-grade education. He responded, "Well, sure. Six, eight, and ten will square any pigpen." We were still in the days when everyone thought and acted in the same familiar world.

Add to this the fact that some Bible translations will use the word *soul* where another says *life*. How are they to be separated or interactive? Then, there are places where the Bible uses *heart*, and we understand that it means the word *mind*. This subject sometimes hovers around the questions of life-support and right-to-die issues. We can think, and there are abundant instructions in God's Word about using our minds, yet there is no mention of the brain anywhere. We do understand that sometimes the word *heart* meant the seat of our emotions. I find it ironic that in today's biblically illiterate, spiritually starved culture, we can still hear this ancient usage on all sides of us: "I love you with all my heart," "I thank you from the bottom of my heart," "In your heart you know it's true." I believe if anyone hears the invitation "You need to give your heart to Jesus," they would really know what it means even if they have no idea who Jesus is.

Our religious talk can confuse even our little ones. On the way home from church one Christmas, our four-year-old granddaughter said to her parents, "I don't understand. Our teacher brought a cake today, and we sang 'Happy Birthday' to Jesus. Now if I have Jesus in my heart, and the cake is in my belly, how is he going to get any of the cake?" How would you explain it to her? How would you explain it to an adult?

What the Bible Doesn't Tell Us

Another significant way the results of new studies made a major impact on the world was new research into the workings of the brain and how we think. This is of huge importance because it directly concerns the whole focus of God's Word, especially as it relates to understanding what it actually says. It became possible to develop instruments and procedures that could probe and record what is really going on inside our skull. Physicians had been probing the brain since at least the nineteenth century, but the limits of their facilities and instruments kept them from observing more than is visible with a microscope. The only way we could tell what people had in mind and made them act the way they do, from the very beginning, was to observe the words and behavior of individuals and groups. This has always been of keen interest to the church as well as to the whole field of mental and spiritual health. We took into account their background, their general intelligence, the homes in which they were raised, additional patterns of their family, their religious background, and any other clues available. There was really no way to look inside a person's head to see what was going on. By the 1950s though, it was easier to look into another realm of creation that had been invisible since the beginning of time.

The human brain consists of about one hundred billion cells called neurons. We are told that most of our other body cells have a limited shelf life of about seven years. God made us so that renewal occurs as an ongoing process so now, in effect, we have developed a new body in that length of time. Not so with the shelf life of our permanent brain; it was made to last for keeps. As we get older, some neurons do wither away but, even if you are older, you probably still have the biggest percentage of those you were born with.

From the day we are born, our individual brain experiences and records everything according to its own system. Then it governs how we think and act according to the way it understands and interprets everything with the limits of its God-given ability. I believe this is crucial to our search for any truth because each one of us will give account to God for ourselves as individuals.

"For the Word of God is sharper than any double-edged sword; it penetrates even dividing soul and spirit, joints and marrow; it judges the attitudes of the heart" (Heb. 4:12). Recent discoveries on how our minds work and how we learn things can be helpful in the church's search for how to proclaim this truth as relevant to what we experience in our modern world. God's spiritual realm touches every fiber of our being, spirit, heart, soul, mind, and body with promise and retribution through his perfect truth. Today, we know what is really happening inside us more than the writer of Hebrews could. Back then, they could not see more than the surface of the joints and marrow or any other part they could cut open to make visible. Some of the differences in our doctrines also come from our different understandings of soul and spirit.

Did you ever hear someone say "How could anyone look at that beautiful sunset sky and not believe in God?" Or "Every time we welcome an innocent newborn child into the world, we surely must believe that the God-given miracle of life is still going on?" Comments such as these are certainly valid and are statements of our faith. For instance, who would say, "Look how sunlight refracts the light spectrum through the prism of three hundred billion droplets of water so they will produce a pattern on my retinas so my brain can put them into such an amazing sight?" It's not the same. Or what about "How can you look at this totally helpless bundle of three hundred trillion living cells with every cell assigned to its appointed task, equipped with the ability to grow, to adapt, and to handle challenges and hardships of life for the next one hundred years and not believe in God?" These are both faith statements. My point is that, even though we know and take for granted that everything is created by God, all our usual emotional and spiritual sense tends to stop on the outside surfaces of our visible world.

15
Ancient Truth—
Modern Appearance

The Total Person

Jesus said, "For I came down from heaven, not to do my own will but the will of Him that sent Me" (John 6:38). By extension, his life and deeds as God, incarnate in a human body, practically make perfect truth a synonym for the Will of God. This means behind his every word and action, the motive is that of a good shepherd leading his flock. We follow in our halting, stumbling fashion with Satan continually under our feet pretending to be a friendly pet trying to push us off the straight and narrow path. But perfect truth is our sure defense calling each one of us forward by name (John 10:3). Even while our minds and hearts are exposed to the influence of the gods of this world, every cell in our body, every neuron in our brain, every synapse in every nerve circuit, every fiber of our being, and our every sense of who we are is being quietly led toward kingdom goals. As the Holy Spirit leads us, the depressing practices of a falling world always try to drag our spirits downward. Perfect truth possessing all authority in heaven and earth (Matt. 28:19) is pleased to maintain our bodies as temples of the living God.

You have probably heard this statement, "Among the billions of people on earth, no two individuals have the same fingerprints." This, in itself, is a faith statement because it has never been proven. This "truth" though, has been accepted to the degree that it can literally mean the difference between a life or death sentence to someone on trial in a courtroom. Today's use of DNA testing goes far beyond the limits of fingerprinting to demonstrate that we are all unique. How much more unlikely is it that two people can ever have identical memories or identical reasoning processes in regard to anything? How could two individuals process the same data and have the same impressions or arrive at identical conclusions?

God's Handiwork within Our Personal World

"The heavens declare the glory of God; and the firmament sheweth his handiwork" (Ps. 19:1).

This has been a truth the church has proclaimed from the beginning. We have known this truth for twenty centuries. Who has ever felt prompted to loudly proclaim that God has also shown his glory in the work of his hands in the amazing worlds of atomic science and electronics? Surely, there are many who have done so with thanksgiving. This is one of the reasons for writing this book. An unwitting neglect of fresh spiritual studies about what modern science was doing has gradually led to the painful disconnect that now exists between the church of Jesus Christ and twenty-first-century society. Who would have thought, seventy-five years ago, that there would be a way to treat cancer and sometimes even to cure it? Yet things like radiation and chemotherapy are now part of our regular vocabulary. Not too long ago, "hardening of the arteries" was just something to accept as a person got older. Conventional wisdom, therefore, had it that your blood pressure should be one hundred plus your age. Extra pressure was required to get through those rigid places. MRIs, CT scans, sonograms, heart catheterizations, and a host of other developments have helped add years to lives as they discovered the culprit was cholesterol. I speak from experience as well as the ability to share what I have learned from others.

As God reveals more information, we benefit in many ways from improved health care. Think about this. Has anyone ever been led in worship to rise and proclaim, "Praise the Lord of the heavens with songs and dancing. Raise the sound of the trumpet and cymbal. For he has created the heavens and the earth, the cattle and birds. He has given us the gamma rays that attack and kill the dreaded cancer cells. He is perfect truth in the ear-splitting sounds of flying electrons trying to find their way home inside a CT scan. His omnipresence carries gospel preaching to the ends of the earth via satellite, and now all the data stored in The Cloud belongs to him!" It sounds irreverent, but it fits the style of the psalmist. And no matter how much we are able to do humanly, God is always the healer. This is the one truth that has not changed since the beginning. Since Jesus had healing high on his list of actions, there is a powerful incentive to maintain our faith in the great physician even as we learn more.

Two Dimensions of the Cross

The cross points in two directions. The vertical points to our relationship with God; the horizontal points in the same way to our fellow human beings.

And so, we go out into the world with a Bible under one arm and a loaf of bread under the other.

The church has cared about the spiritual and physical well-being of individuals from the beginning. The Gospel soon moves on from preaching salvation to demonstrations of God's love. Sometimes our witness may call for a cup of cold water (Matt. 10:42). At other times, it may be something more stressful. "Therefore, if thine enemy hunger, feed him" (Rom. 12:20). Outreach ministries have included hospitals, leprosariums, children's homes, and other endeavors. How could all these beneficial things have occurred without the inspiration of perfect truth working in our midst? It follows then that we should be interested in newer things that research has made possible to learn what may be helpful in all godly efforts.

If there is no God-given spiritual potential in us, then our striving and goals are on an animal level of self-preservation. We're all in the same boat—survival of the fittest. Everything we do on this accursed ground, even cooperating for the common good, is part of building our own tower to heaven. Presumably, the superior among us will rise to the top. I saw a cartoon showing two worms crawling up out of a grave. The one looks at the other and says, "Top of the food chain. Hah!"

Perfect truth, as the ever-active power of God's will that maintains balance in every action, is on display all around us. Light reciprocates with dark so we can sleep. Hoist a sail and the wind can move a ship against the resistance of the water. The piston interacts with power released from gasoline, and we transfer our work to machines. The waterwheel responds to the force of the current, and we have power. We apply brakes to a moving vehicle, and it stops. We know you don't use a sledgehammer to drive thumbtacks, and the engine for an eighteen-wheeler does not fit into the family sedan.

Spiritual Guidance for Spiritual Beings

For example, Romans 7:14–8:2 gives us an important reason why we should bring the invisible worlds of science into our study of religious doctrine and all spiritual reality. Here is a real live demonstration of perfect truth in the center of all our dilemmas. Paul is describing exactly how the contest between doing good or evil involves our body, mind, and spirit. His struggle is not only spiritual; it involves the thought cells in the brain, the urges of the worldly cells in his body, and the central nervous system. Brain cells, on-off switches in nerve circuits and blood pressure cannot exist in his thinking. All Paul knows is that it makes life miserable. "O wretched man that I am. Who shall deliver me from the body of this death? I thank God through our Lord Jesus Christ. For the law of the Spirit of life in Christ Jesus has set me free from the law of sin and death" (Rom. 7:24–8:2). A friend of mine told me that when she was two, she and her parents were visiting relatives. She misbehaved somehow and her mother disciplined her. In the process, her mother asked her why she did wrong when she knew better. Her answer, "Me wants to be good but myself won't let me." It seems that Paul is sharing a truth that curses us from childhood. Amazing grace is more than comforting words; it reaches down inside and takes hold of you.

Guidance Needed for Unique Change

It is important that we consider new applications of God's Word in relation to modern knowledge about the world of the intellect and how the physical part of our makeup reciprocates with the mental and emotional systems. This combination of actions has much to do with our health and well-being. Educators and others have been telling us for years that the developing brains of children are being rewired by the electronic visual images that are a big part of their lives. This influence, combined with new teaching methods made possible through electronics, has been contributing to the problem of a widening generation gap. I believe this influence on the minds of people for many years helped lead to the great gulf existing between the church and the world.

Teachers and others in our congregations are well aware of efforts the schools and other child-related industries are making to adjust to the changing times. We often copy their methods to learn how to adjust to this shift in culture. Ministers accommodate messages and refine or completely redesign worship styles and music to connect with this changing scene. The problem is that all this is only dealing with symptoms of the spiritual illness. Society, with all its material goals for a limited lifespan, creates its curriculum to help students to become successful in this material world. The church has more than just a subject to teach; we have a saving gospel for the whole person that will save their souls and teach them how to apply themselves to all those other lessons and prepare for eternity. We have perfect truth.

16
Connect Sunday to Monday

Traditional Believers among Nontraditional Believers

A modern comment: "I'm spiritual, but I'm not religious." Do not take this lightly, especially if a younger person says it; they are serious. A question remains though—what does this "spirituality" mean? I've been told that, sometimes, it's shorthand for "I don't need the church" and may well be. Even if it is, there is an acknowledgment that life is more than that which we can see, hear, smell, taste, and feel.

A real problem for the modern church throughout the country is how to show a more direct live connection between our Sunday worship experience and our daily lives. For those who are older, it was easier and seemed more natural in years gone by. In the past, society, in general, accepted that there was a day set apart with spiritual importance. Modern generations in our culture are losing contact with the church, and part of it is because they don't see it as relevant. Those without any church background or religious instruction in the home have no spiritual basis to make connections. Those who have been brought up in the nurture and admonition of the Lord (Eph. 6:4) find it harder to feel any real spiritual connection to their world outside of church. My conclusion is that because the church's path goes one direction, and modern science goes another, we have lost the active contact that was very real a hundred years ago. A curious thing about it is that, at this same time, millions of our members are actively involved in and feel at home in this other "new world." Perhaps the younger ones need to sit down with the older ones and try to find the missing connections, not just to ask, "How can we close the generation gap?" but "How can we understand that God is acting in and around us?" How can we cross the spiritual gap that gets wider between us with every generation? That was already a question when Solomon was writing Proverbs.

A key reason behind this whole project is to encourage development of twenty-first-century theologies that will find perfect truth in the invisible worlds discovered in the last century. Before we can learn the new language of our new environment, I suggest that we begin with what we already have in common with the different age groups who already are with us in the church. The following is an example from my own experience and what I was taught.

Reconnect Sunday With Monday

As a youngster, I go to Sunday school and church and learn there are words like *salvation, sin, grace, judgment, heaven, hell, doctrines, creeds, teachings, faith statements, miracles, sacraments, miracles, sins,* and heresies. We learn what they mean through teaching and preaching from portions of scripture. These are words handed down through the years based on the Word of God and derived from experience of the church. They are all based on our faith. Some things we can see with our eyes. They don't have to be proven because many of them are visible. Some things are self-evident and need no explanation. Some are understood through faith. Please note: these references are not necessarily faith statements but part of the illustration.

On Monday I go to school. There we have words like *scientific method, phenomenon, theories, formula, theorems, aberrations, axioms,* and *corollaries,* laws that needed no proof because they are self-evident truths, laws of probability. Some similarities to religious language are fairly plain. Notice any need for faith somewhere along this line? We believe in things that are too small to see in a microscope. We understand that, as students, we are dabbling our toes in the simplest areas of science. There is much more. We have never seen a jet plane or heard the word *television.*

In those days, we had faith in our teachers and thoroughly understood the world around us. Actually, it was the same world our grandparents knew as did their grandparents before them. Above all, when we went to church and Sunday school, we had no thought that we were thinking about a different environment. The ministers, the teachers, and all the older members knew what the young people were learning because they had learned from the same books. The church and science were still on the same page. I believe the church is still on that page.

Times Change

While the visible arenas of nature and science were revealing natural truths through our physical senses, the church was rightfully proclaiming spiritual truths from the Bible. By the mid-twentieth century, this pattern allowed our concern for the truths of material substance to fade away, except for our physical health and well-being. However, the new truths science discovered that were not revealed via the senses began to rapidly change our lives. So we now have various incentives for looking into God's word to discover what it reveals about the secrets of this post-Christian age. One very important reason is so that we can proclaim the gospel in twenty-first century language with new understandings of how our ears hear it and the mind and soul process it.

One time, before computers were even on the scene, I heard a professor say, "The best thing you can do for the students in your classroom is to give them a built-in fool-proof garbage detector." Surely, his advice is as appropriate today as it was back then. Beginning in 1950, television was probably the main device from outside that had much influence on the children. Today's toddlers begin with more elaborate devices. At what age should we be able to teach them God's purpose for their lives? And how can we take into account the invisible alterations taking place in their brains? Even if you grew up with similar toys and tools, how can you make allowance for the mutations that occur in each generation? These are hard questions. I hope you can look for opportunities to follow up on this and add what you already know. Perhaps compare your faith journey with that of your parents' and then that of a younger generation. Learn from the children. How can they connect Jesus's comparing us to sheep following a shepherd while they have no concept of either? How do you do it? Where does your spirit of worship flow over into your attitude about your work? Where does it connect with what you are actually doing?

17
Widening Generation Gaps

Learning Is a Two-Way Street

One major factor in the widening generation gap, especially in church, is the way we communicate and fail to communicate at the same time. Now surely is the time for clergy and laity—women, men, youth, children—to step into the gap. Proclaiming the Word depends on using language that is understood. Part of the disconnect is the result of rapidly changing language in schools and the workplace.

This is about more than just language. New words, abbreviations, and symbols are cropping up all the time, and anyone who follows daily communication, especially working with computers and so on, keeps up with it. I mean beyond that. You and I learn new words all our lives. This is an issue where the quotation applies, "The meanings of words lie not just in the words themselves but in the meaning we attach to them" (Antoine de Saint-Exupéry). That's why we refer to one's native tongue. The influx of new words and symbols used by young people are foreign to their grandparents and can be vague to parents. Consider the fact that they're growing up in a fast-moving world, which means our old words do sound different. This is especially important when sharing the good news with them because faith is not taught, it's caught. It has been pointed out that when our children were little, we spelled words so they wouldn't know what we were talking about. Today, many adults have no idea what their offspring are saying to their friends. Children and youth are learning a fresh native tongue with all it means for them. We need intergeneration interpreters, and perhaps, you could be one. If I go to visit a foreign land with a visitor's language handbook to help me get around, I can survive and even enjoy some small talk. But if I've gone there to share the Bible's good news and never learn their language, forget it. At Pentecost, people from many lands heard the gospel for the first time, but they all heard it in their own tongue. To this day, I feel that churches are seeking to be faithful to the great commandment and recognize the need to relate to all people in ways they understand.

The biblical worldviews held by believers are as varied as there are denominations or sects. Besides that, every individual will have their own faith and understanding of the gospel. This book is not commenting on your beliefs in any way but is to help find ways to connect the Bible lessons of antiquity to the post-Christian culture of today. Our ancestors developed traditional theologies that were tried and tested through perfect truth interacting with the world, and we have inherited their values. Today, the gods of this world are moving so rapidly that we can't sit and wait for someone to show us how to shine the light of the gospel. "For everyone that doeth evil hateth the light; neither cometh to the light that his deeds should be reproved" (John 3:20).

In God's plan for creation, perfect truth is working constantly to balance everything in every age group to fulfill his will. If you think my assessment of this picture has any merit, the following may be helpful.

JOHN E. EASH

Teaching Our Children's Children

When languages move into an area, they tend to evolve into useful local dialects. This is what I believe has been happening rapidly for the last seventy years. Language, grammar and vocabulary used to be taught in the schools. Change occurred slowly and was modified as needed by language teachers and dictionary printers. Today, vocabulary is invented by people outside school systems and is modified on the run by all who are learning how to use it. Cursive writing is on its way to the museum. No matter how rapidly things change, though, you will at least have some continuity in transit wherever you have contact within the faith community and/or your world outside of it. Perfect truth is in the reciprocating back-and-forth exchange of knowledge and expression of emotions that move us along our individual journeys. Perhaps you can step into the gaps wherever fits best and try for some more back-and-forth understanding. It's time for all hands on deck!

Here might be a language pattern we can adapt from real life. Having grown up in a coal-mining area with imported labor, I have seen this often. The newcomers spoke their mother tongue but learned English. The children learned both languages and often translated for their parents. The grandchildren learned varying amounts of the old language or perhaps none. The next generation speaks only English. The only thing is that this process takes fifty years, and God has no grandchildren.

Whenever science, mathematics, or other disciplines discuss something new, it can add a new word to their language or affect attitudes toward something else. This can mean a subtle change in language. If it is important enough, especially in health care, it influences many people. When any company introduces a new product for consumers, they hope the brand name will become a household word, like thermos bottle and scotch tape. All of us are used to this kind of change and understand how it works. As our vocabulary grows, it shifts to make room for the word and how its meaning fits in with all the others. Meanwhile in the church, our doctrines are neatly contained in their old familiar word patterns. In days gone by, you could sit down with someone, perhaps a stranger, who knew nothing about the Bible and could explain what it means. Living in the same world meant you had a common understanding of life and what was going on in peoples' lives around you. Today, if you discuss scripture with someone twenty-five years younger or older than yourself, it often doesn't seem to make the same connections.

Anyone born over fifty years ago is now traveling in a land where new words are appearing all the time, old words are dropping out as well as what they stood for. I do subscribe to the old maxim that times change but not the Bible's message. We simply adjust our methods. This book is about more than just updating methods. It used to be that parents lamented the generation gap, which we would eventually outgrow. When I became an adult, my parents and I could understand each other perfectly, which couldn't happen ten years earlier. Today our children are growing up in a culture that shifts direction a little farther each year. We have all heard, "If you talk the talk, you have to walk the walk." You also need to know the talk. It's hard to know how and when the influence of any outside interest will affect the thoughts of children. One Sunday, a pastor I know was asked by a first-time acolyte, "Should I sit up front or in the bleachers?"

The youngster may already be thinking that church is for spectators.

Understandings of what is meaningful in life and the values of a personal faith have been going through deeply felt changes for quite some time.

18
Preserving God's Word

Permanent Book, Disappearing Bookcases

What is the best way to preserve the Bible, God's written Word, when it is disappearing as we know it?

"All scripture is inspired of God" (2 Tim. 2:16) This does not say that the meaning of God's Word is contained solely in the written words and printed characters themselves but in the spiritual message preserved in the meaning of the words. Printed in many different languages, God's Word lies quietly on inky surfaces ready to speak his message to the eyes, ears, and hearts of all who read or hear. The paper pages and leather binding hold it all together, shielding it from harmful light and other aspects of the environment that can damage it. Spinning within their tightly prescribed orbits, trillions of neutrons and electrons cling to one another as they carry out their appointed duty. Holy Spirit teaching and preaching from this familiar printed book will continue to bring its saving message to the lost; but the book is becoming an endangered species. Changing communications require us to learn more ways to connect to the world. The Bible still is our visible evidence of God's Word for mankind. We need doctrines and understanding of how perfect truth is seeking God's will via electronic methods.

Millions of readers extend a reverence toward the Bible that is not given to any other book. This love is tied directly to its role as the repository of God's Word. Whenever there is reference to "the Word of God as revealed in Scripture," we instantly think of the Bible in print. This is so important to some believers that their feelings about it may vary as to a specific version or translation. Also, for some, legitimate pulpit reading from the Bible must be straight from the printed book itself. I knew one pastor who had a minor to-do over this. Rather than turn back and forth to refer to a couple of verses that he wanted to include, he printed them out and laid the paper on the pulpit. To some of the congregation, that wasn't real Bible reading. No matter how we regard the Bible, though, it is not an object of worship. It commands special respect because it is the voice of God. It reminds us that we live under his mercy and judgment. It contains the message of salvation through Jesus Christ. It is a tangible sign that the old, old story is alive and well. I personally don't see how to impress this sense of biblical authority upon a generation that will not have books. This is something that refreshed theology regarding present-day discoveries may be able to do. I hope you can be part of that process regardless of your age.

My Own Bible

The Bible, as we know it, earned the affectionate name "the Good Book" many years ago; but it is really recent history. The Bible did not come to us overnight. Since ancient days, Christians have recorded their message via any means available to them. The New Testament writers recorded their inspirations on the writing materials of the day. During years of persecution, believers depicted Bible scenes on the walls of the Roman catacombs. Later on, church buildings appeared where sculpture, architecture and painting became visual aids. Then printing came of age which slowly led to modern mass production.

In lots of homes, the Bible became a history of family milestones. Births, weddings, deaths were recorded there. Churches placed oversize editions with large print for use as pulpit Bibles. Moving further into the twentieth century, individual Bibles became common and were found in many homes. Small editions of the New Testament could be carried in a purse or pocket as tangible reminders of God's presence. During World War II, many soldiers carried New Testaments, often in the breast pocket. A special issue was available with steel covers. Bibles served as gifts for special occasions. I received my own personal Bible for a birthday present shortly after I was baptized. In many churches, spring graduation became a time to recognize seniors and crown their achievements with a copy of God's Word. This may bring to your mind a particular Bible you remember from home or the church or perhaps your own. In other developing parts of the world, the need for Bibles has opened up an important field for translators and missionaries.

The Bible, as we know it in its familiar form, will remain as our focus of faith for a long time to come. But at the same time, the handwriting is on the wall in disappearing ink. The Good Book is with us twenty-four hours a day, and a touch of an "app" brings these words to us in an instant. However, instead of sitting in a place of distinction (i.e., the "coffee table"), it is buried in an electronic device amidst a myriad of information and distractions. When Paul told the Athenians, "In him we live and move and have our being," he was proclaiming spiritual truth. Today, we can present this spiritual truth as a fact. It can be demonstrated. It is literally in the atmosphere.

When I read the scriptures on my cell phone, I simply read as though the message is in a printed copy. Any other scriptures that come to mind as I read appear in printed words on pages in my memory cells. Anyone whose Bible-reading has been confined solely to electronic media can't do that; they can't "see" pages. Their thought patterns and brain-cell impressions appear via a new language that has been in the making for half a century.

Ministers in thousands of churches will continue to hold the Bible aloft as the Word of God and with good reason for a long time to come. Millions of the faithful will continue to revere its form and its message. As more of us are beginning to use laptops and other electronic devices in the pulpit, though, it is not the same as simply switching from one version of the Bible to another. When I go to read the Bible in any translation, I have a sense of Holy Spirit omnipresence in the whole book. God's Word is preserved in every jot and tittle, every letter, every comma, every period. The words are combined in printed language that registers in my brain cells the same way I've been learning all my life, the same way they've been programmed since I was a little child. I know the identical word is revealed in my laptop, but somehow, it feels different coming from the same screen where I print my grocery list.

The Word in New Forms

Another reason we need a fresh breeze to stir up our old familiar doctrines is that the generation gap perceived by the church is a far more serious problem than it seems to be for a secular society. As new knowledge comes into the workplace and new products appear on the market, they are accepted at face value and bundled as such. Whether they are good or not will be decided by the general public and how they respond in the marketplace. Public opinions, philosophies, subjects in school, changes in the workplace, and other things that influence our habits are worked out within the rules of a common largely commercial culture. The everyday world seems to no longer be aware that there is a Bible. Most church theologies are based on how we believe God has worked with human beings from the very beginning. It applies the Bible to history and experiences that happened before the twentieth century. Society today seems to have little interest in history, and its daily experience has changed a lot since 1950. Examples of this are often evident in reruns of old family situation programs on television. We need fresh insights to break through the new barriers the gods of this world have erected.

Finding how to let new light shine on our search for spiritual meaning in the vast invisible areas of God's creation means starting out with what we can already see and already believe. This means thinking about how faith fits in with God's active presence in the fast-moving world of electronics. Jesus said to Nicodemus, "I have spoken to you of earthly things, and you do not believe; how then will you believe if I speak of heavenly things?" (John 3:12). We still have a lot to learn about both.

One example to consider is that Sunday morning's worship service can be livestreamed or recorded to make it available for you to play at home on your compact disc (CD) player. I could also say that it is made available online or on Facebook. The spiritual setting would be the same, but a CD is easier for me to illustrate. You start the process. The worship leader reads the scripture and, as you listen, the spirit of perfect truth arranges the continuity of corporate worship as God's Word is being read from the printed page. The sense and meaning of the words register with understanding in your heart and soul. Whenever the minister says "will you bow your head with me while we pray," you bow your head. You are together in the spirit at that moment and agreement with God and the intention of Sunday's prayer. When the congregation sings, you sing or hum along in your spirit as memory calls up familiar melodies. It is such a blessing that a few days later you decide to listen to it again. Will you again be joined in spirit the same way you were the first time? What if it is really only the sermon you wanted to hear, and you fast forward through the other parts? Is the spiritual reality the same on every occasion?

Here are questions the church could have started to raise one hundred years ago when sound recording was invented; perhaps they did raise questions of which I am unaware. The same questions may well have applied to the broadcasting industry as radio and television became important factors in many church efforts to reach the public.

New Form, Age-Old Truths

The following comments and questions are framed around my belief that perfect truth directly participates in every facet of the recording process and in the replaying. Perfect truth is balancing the actions of every molecule, atom, electron, and neutron with the equipment and people taking part. The spiritual elements in the scene described above involve the speaker's thoughts, his vocal abilities, sound waves from his lips to the recording device. In the same way the music involves the voices in song, instrumental interlude, and everything else in that service. All the sounds from the worship service, including the words read from the Bible, will be projected from the recording to the listeners' ears. There, all the elements will make it audible, and the messages relayed to his brain will make appropriate spiritual connections with his soul.

Modern science can follow the sequence of events and tell us exactly how it works according to God-given natural laws. But we know it is more than a merely mechanical process no matter how complicated it becomes mentally or physically. These are spiritual circumstances, and God is present as we worship him in spirit and in truth. Sound engineers and experts, who know how our mind functions, can only go so far. How valuable is the fact that every word of every prayer, the sermon, the hymns, the music of the choir, and any instruments are permanently imprinted upon an inanimate plastic object? Every sound is electronically etched in the proper sequence ready to project its divine message every time it is called upon. Does this make the disc holy in the same way we say Holy Bible?

Additionally, if the service is put on Facebook or online, where is the Word of God when nobody is watching? Is it somewhere in the cloud or in cyberspace? What about the Bible messages in television and radio waves flying through space looking for receptors to enter? If we look into these elements from the standpoint of what the Bible tells us about creation and how we are to deal with it and how we are to live in relationships with each other, what does it say? "In him we live and move and have our being" (Acts 17:28). I have been taught that he is as near as the air we breathe. "You are the temple of the Holy Spirit"

(Rom. 6:19). These are deep subjects that are more than we can really comprehend from our traditional teachings. How do they relate to a world of the new circumstances that are touching our lives?

19
What Will a Real Bible Look Like?

The Word Meets the World

The early disciples turned the world upside down with the good news that Jesus is our Savior. He died on a cross so that we might have eternal life. Through faith in him, our sins are forgiven, and we are saved from death and hell and shall be with God forever. As the Holy Spirit indwells us, we are living temples (1 Cor. 3:16). As God's people, we are living stones built into a spiritual house (1 Pet. 2:5). The early disciples proclaimed the gospel throughout the Roman Empire centuries before the Bible was completed. Our role is to penetrate the ungodly resistance of our world in a way that will communicate this same gospel with all the means that we have. The Bible promises, "My word shall not return unto me void" (Isa. 55:11). The message of Christ's death and resurrection is the center and foundation of faith. We need to proclaim this faith once delivered unto the saints (Jude 1:3) using a language and a medium they understand. Today's inventions give us access to communicate the message easier and in more convenient ways than ever such as with laptops and cell phones. But right here is one of the real reasons why we need doctrines that help us use these new methods to the best advantage. They bring a new set of opportunities to share our doctrines of the Bible as holy, pure, and dedicated to sacred uses. It does pose a question as to the actual physical relationship of the word of God to the surroundings.

We know that God's word is sharper than a two-edged sword and, like a surgeon's scalpel, searches our hearts and minds, judging whatever it finds there (Heb. 4:12). But what about the word actually printed on the Bible's pages? How do we justify mingling its contents with the sin and filth growing unchecked in our electronic world? The Bible recorded in laptops and cell phones is thoroughly immersed in their electronic environment that is at home and participates in the most wicked thinking and attitudes on the planet. On the one hand, one might say, "But that's different. It has nothing to do with the Word of God itself. Plus, our intentions for his message are honorable." But on the other hand, what if we regard the Scriptures in the light of the Bible as described elsewhere in this work with the regard that makes it the Good Book? It would seem to be on a spiritual level different from other objects.

The Word and the Modern World

For the record, laptops and cell phones themselves are not the issue. Thousands of spirit-filled preachers and teachers faithfully read the Bible and teach the Word of God from these devices. They are inanimate electronic vehicles that preserve and present the same message contained in any other medium. It probably won't be many years before they outnumber printed Bibles in the pulpit. Here is the point from a theological perspective: Lots of scripture, especially in the Old

Testament, is never read at the dinner table. There are many passages of scripture that could be seen as adult material. They are simply accepted as part of God's message. Lots of times they are rearranged for pulpit use because of the little ears in the pews. Now consider this, a friend gives you a Bible and says, "Someone wrote some really filthy stuff in the margins but don't worry, that doesn't hurt what's inside. Also, wherever the Bible describes some steamy scenes, they drew obscene pictures, just ignore them." What would be your first emotional (spiritual) response? To some, perhaps, it wouldn't make much difference. But there are lots of folks that wouldn't touch it with a ten-foot pole. How do you think you would react?

Television and radio are another category, but admittedly, that may be only to a degree. I have no control over television broadcasting, but I can understand how it works. There are lots of G-rated programs, interesting shows, and religious programs I can choose. What I don't select has nothing to do with my spiritual status. My laptop and cell phone are something else. My fingerprint opens up many websites and accounts. When the activity on my device is analyzed, this data is called my footprint. This footprint shows where I have been and predicts where I am likely to be going. This creates an electronic memory. Those electronic memories are about email, text messages, personal conversations by phone, or in print, sometimes funny, sometimes sad. It remembers what I google. The tracks also mingle with everything coming through Facebook which can be very good, especially with friends. It can also be newscasts, helpful data, hateful, X-rated, or otherwise, objectionable.

JOHN E. EASH

The Word in My Private World

At present, I can think of no scripture that gives specific guidance for this issue. Moses proclaims the name of the Lord and his greatness (Deut. 32:3). According to Psalm 1, the godly meditate in the law of the Lord. Jesus gives teachings on sowing and reaping in kingdom parables (Matt. 13:24–30; Mark 4:26–32). Paul advises thinking about things that are true, honest, pure, and the like (Phil. 4:26–32). Something in these passages, or others you can think of, may help you find an opening for this issue. In any case, I believe perfect truth flows through the situation. Regardless how it eventually plays out, electronic devices probably will totally dominate all nonpersonal communications.

We realize that the scriptures are our sole connection to the faith of Abraham, the life and resurrection of Jesus, and the beginnings of the church. There is no other record. The dilemma is, if we need to maintain the word of God where everyone can see it, how do we do it?

We control what goes into our "personal data." We can block certain people from information on our Facebook "wall," and we can delete or block certain emails, etc. This is not unlike the control we try to take over our own hearts and minds. God's spoken word remains powerful and unchanged even if we try to twist it to fit our own circumstances.

One way that believers have committed scriptures to memory over hundreds of years is by setting them to music. The words of the great hymns of the church were often directly taken from the Word of God. Modern-day churches are often "packed" on Sunday mornings, and they are singing these same scriptures to more current and trendy styles of music.

Even these types of churches need to keep this new and fresh. What was popular in the early 2000s is now outdated twenty years later.

As daunting as we may find this issue, its importance will vary according to our individual belief. The Bible itself indicates that the Holy Spirit will find a way. In 2 Timothy 2:9, Paul, who is in chains, writes, "The word of God is not bound." The Word of God cannot and will not be kept under lock and key no matter how hard the forces of this world try to keep it out of sight. Hallelujah!

20
God's Word Renews Truth

Ancient Problem—Modern Solution

It can be hard to realize that the true relationship between the early church and the world outside of it has never changed. We know it hasn't because the present on-going activity of the Holy Spirit sustains perfect truth uniting them with us. Our way of life has almost nothing in common with their ancient culture, but they can teach you and me a lot just from their appreciation of their own history. Read Acts 4:13–31; I think it's a must. Their attitude and expectations in prayer are amazing. They are aware that what they are facing was already going on a thousand years before their time. King David was fully acquainted with it. In fact, he was inspired to warn us all that what goes around comes around. Once again, prophecies were coming true. Christ's enemies are still stirring up people all around conspiring with leaders to get official support, inciting Jews and Gentiles to revive hatred, anything—including murder—to stop the gospel. But these early believers go right over the heads of the enemy with fervent prayer. They appeal to God who has created heaven, earth, the sea, and everything in them. They know all about Moses, David and Goliath, Samson, Gideon, and Elijah; now it's their turn. They simply call upon God to help them to go out and show what he can do "by the name of thy Holy Child, Jesus".

Study the Forest, Not Only the Trees

I heard an anthropologist say that two of the hardest things for us to change as adults are our earliest religious teachings and childhood food patterns. You may want to check out that idea with yourself and family. As youngsters, many of us were taught to hold a spirit of reverence toward the Bible as the Word of God. That did not mean that a volume of the Good Book has a separate holiness in itself or merits worship; rather, it is different from other books simply because of its content and purpose. Most Bibles are printed to be handled; they are to be read and used in ways that help us learn and share the good news. There are special editions of the Bible designed for their holy symbolism. They often are seen on coffee tables, the entrance to a business, special places in a church, etc. These copies are intended to maintain their appearance indefinitely. Bibles intended for reading, studying, teaching, and preaching will wear out, along with their handwritten notes, underlined texts, stained and torn pages, and duct-taped covers. But even though it is a material object, the Bible seems to be different from other publications. A long time ago, I was taught that the preacher in the pulpit should not treat the Bible like a butcher with a meat cleaver.

As we seek perfect truth in God's Word, we must keep in mind something that's so familiar we hardly notice it. Dividing the Bible into chapters and verses gave us an efficient way to reference passages and help memorize our favorite verses. That is how I still do it. Each book of the Bible, though, except Psalms, was written as a unit without divisions. About one thousand years ago, a printer came up with the brilliant idea of dividing them up into chapters to give it an index. Several centuries later, another printer was led to fine-tune the idea by cutting the chapters into smaller bits called verses. When we look into scripture for truths to define our doctrines and guide our faith journey, it is important to consider its full message in proper context. It is possible to isolate a statement of belief because of a printer's punctuation.

It has been said, "A Bible that's falling apart usually belongs to someone who isn't." One instructor told us, "If I want to know what version of the Bible you prefer, I'll ask you to let me see your Bible. I won't look at the cover. The most-worn pages will tell me."

Raise the Roof

Sometimes, people are eager to make contact with Jesus but, hindered by the crowds, come up with their own solutions. Zaccheus climbed a tree so he could see over their heads. A woman who needed relief from a chronic hemorrhage simply pushed through the people till she could get within arm's reach of him. Blind Bartimaeus shouted till Jesus heard him above the hubbub of the crowd. Sometimes though, they needed help. The gospels record such a time where four men literally broke into the house where Jesus was. They tore up the roof. They didn't open it just wide enough so Jesus could see their patient. They moved enough tiles so they could let their paralyzed friend down through the roof into his presence; then their part was done (Mark 2:3–12; Luke 5:18–20). Both accounts of this miracle state that Jesus sees their faith, forgives the man of his sins, and heals him.

I include these events as illustrations because the progress of modern science is making it harder for younger generations to realize that they have a need for the gospel message in the first place. The idols of the world are offering a paradise on earth. The principles of a godless society speak a language that has nothing to do with the tried-and-true language of familiar church doctrine that has lifted up perfect truth for centuries. Millions, like sheep without a shepherd, are not purposely fleeing from him; they just don't realize a shepherd exists. They need help.

21
Invitation to Action

One Body, One Mission, One Truth

A major hope for this book is that it will open up a mutual search for perfect truth helpful to all believers. Although there are some areas where the church does seem to be making a difference, most of society seems to be heading into the future with little taste for any words from God. Jesus saw the multitudes scattered abroad as sheep having no shepherd (Matt. 9:36). The harvest truly is plenteous, and the laborers are few (Matt. 9:37). It is important then that we keep searching the Bible to grasp those vital teachings that apply to our present generation, not just those that confirm our personal faith statements and doctrines but the foundations of faith that are shared by all. Believers have the message of perfect truth for millions who realize they are living in a world of half-truths and lies but don't know there is another way.

The generation gaps include all ages and every few years get a new name. The older have the experiences while the younger learn only what is new. But a ditch is just as wide no matter which way you need to jump over it. Since the gaps are all about communication, it will take a willingness to hear from both sides.

This work is not intended as a "We have a serious problem, Why doesn't someone do something about it?" Rather, it is to say, "We have a serious problem. Here is something we can try to do." I hope that the ideas and actions proposed have made you aware of what may be best for you. Any place your thinking happens to differ from what you have read may just be the starting point for a positive approach to the problem. The intention of my writing is to stimulate and encourage thinking about God in ways that can help all of us to tell the old familiar story in modern-day language. This is a call for action, not a call for panic. The advice Jesus gave his fishermen disciples, "Launch out into the deep" (Luke 5:4), has been a text for many evangelistic sermons. If we do so, we will need to go deeper than the old charts show. "Because greater is he that is in you, than he that is in the world" (1 John 4:4).

Our faith journey has the promise that Jesus is with us, and he will never leave us or forsake us (Heb. 13:5). Trust the Holy Spirit.

This is not a child's game we are involved in. You and I are called to the arena of a struggle that spells eternal life or death for millions, and their numbers are increasing by the thousands. The apostles are introduced to the plan when Jesus tells them the objectives of the Holy Spirit. "When he comes, he will reprove the world of sin, and of righteousness and of judgment" (John 16:8). That is his method for calling the world to account, and it began at Pentecost. And how does it happen? Are we to be sitting in the bleachers and watching the Spirit at work? I think, rather, that it happens when believers go forth to be the church of Jesus Christ—with our human limitations—to proclaim the kingdom of God. We have the assurance of victory. "And upon this rock I will build my church; and the gates of hell shall not prevail against it" (Matt. 16:18).

There is a place for everyone as we take the Gospel out to the world. You and I have the abilities God has given us and, according to the parables, he really expects us to be responsible for them. They will suit the functions of the body of Christ in his ongoing war with the powers of this world (Matt. 25:15, Rom. 12:6, 1 Cor. 12; Eph. 4:3). Remember the time John told Jesus that they saw someone casting out demons in Jesus's name; they told him to quit because he wasn't in their group. Jesus reversed that decision. He told John not to make the man stop, "Forbid him not; for he that is not against us is for us" (Luke 9:50).

About the Author

The author is an ordained Church of the Brethren minister who, with his late wife, served over forty years in pastoral ministry. Having been involved with their church at local and national levels, as well as inter-church ministries, he has observed how believers tend to function in various settings. Prior to answering the church's call, he was on the national advertising staff of a daily newspaper, working with advertising agencies and other businesses. This experience gave him the opportunity to see how our beliefs can be tested in the everyday life of the world.

He says, "The seed for this book was planted when I was a youngster. I heard the question, 'If all things are possible with God, can he make a stone so big he can't lift it?' Believing that God is omnipotent, I let the seed germinate for years. It finally came to me that the answer is within the perfect truth of God's Word as revealed in Jesus Christ."

He has a BS degree in secondary education, social studies, and is a navy veteran of the Korean War. He and his wife raised four daughters who have their own families. He lives near Johnstown, Pennsylvania, in the area where he grew up.

9 781098 097905